Cambridge English

EMPOWER

PRE-INTERMEDIATE
WORKBOOK
WITH ANSWERS

B1

Peter Anderson

Contents

				Page
Unit 1 Communicating				
1A	Do you play any sports?	**Grammar** Question forms **Vocabulary** Common adjectives		4
1B	I'm really into Facebook	**Grammar** Present simple and present continuous **Vocabulary** Adverbs	**Pronunciation** Long and short vowels	5
1C	It was really nice to meet you	**Everyday English** Greeting people; Ending a conversation	**Pronunciation** Sentence stress	6
1D	I'm sending you some photos	**Reading** An email about a holiday	**Writing skills** Correcting mistakes **Writing** A reply to an email asking about a holiday	7
Reading and listening extension		**Reading** An article about internet dating	**Listening** A conversation about making friends	8
Review and extension		WORDPOWER *like*		9
Unit 2 Travel and Tourism				
2A	We had an adventure	**Grammar** Past simple **Vocabulary** Tourism	**Pronunciation** *-ed* endings	10
2B	Everyone was waiting for me	**Grammar** Past continuous **Vocabulary** Travel collocations	**Pronunciation** Sentence stress: vowel sounds	11
2C	What time's the next train?	**Everyday English** Asking for information in a public place	**Pronunciation** Joining words	12
2D	This city is different, but very friendly	**Reading** A travel blog	**Writing skills** Linking words **Writing** A blog post	13
Reading and listening extension		**Reading** An article about a race	**Listening** A conversation about travel problems	14
Review and extension		WORDPOWER *off*		15
Unit 3 Money				
3A	Have you ever helped a stranger?	**Grammar** Present perfect or past simple **Vocabulary** *make / do / give* collocations		16
3B	I've already spent my salary this month	**Grammar** Present perfect with *just*, *already* and *yet* **Vocabulary** Money		17
3C	Do you have anything cheaper?	**Everyday English** Talking to people in shops	**Pronunciation** Sentence stress	18
3D	We've successfully raised £500	**Reading** An email about raising money for charity	**Writing skills** Paragraphing **Writing** An email to colleagues about a charity	19
Reading and listening extension		**Reading** An article about saving money	**Listening** A conversation about helping people	20
Review and extension		WORDPOWER *just*		21
Unit 4 Social Life				
4A	I'm going to the hairdresser's tomorrow	**Grammar** Present continuous and *going to* **Vocabulary** Clothes and appearance	**Pronunciation** Sound and spelling: *going to*	22
4B	Shall we go to the market?	**Grammar** *will / won't / shall* **Vocabulary** Adjectives: places	**Pronunciation** Sound and spelling: *want* and *won't*	23
4C	Are you doing anything on Wednesday?	**Everyday English** Making arrangements	**Pronunciation** Sentence stress	24
4D	Are you free on Saturday?	**Reading** An email invitation	**Writing skills** Inviting and replying **Writing** A reply to an invitation	25
Reading and listening extension		**Reading** An article about a film director's day	**Listening** A conversation about summer plans	26
Review and extension		WORDPOWER *look*		27
Unit 5 Work				
5A	I have to work long hours	**Grammar** *must / have to / can* **Vocabulary** Work		28
5B	I might get a job today!	**Grammar** *will* and *might* for predictions **Vocabulary** Jobs		29
5C	I'll finish things here, if you want	**Everyday English** Offers and suggestions	**Pronunciation** Sentence stress: vowel sounds	30
5D	I am writing to apply for a job	**Reading** A job advert and a letter	**Writing skills** Organising an email **Writing** A letter applying for a job	31
Reading and listening extension		**Reading** An article about studying and careers	**Listening** A conversation about jobs	32
Review and extension		WORDPOWER *job* and *work*		33
Unit 6 Problems and Advice				
6A	You should have a break	**Grammar** Imperative; *should* **Vocabulary** Verbs with dependent prepositions	**Pronunciation** Sound and spelling: /uː/ and /ʊ/	34
6B	I was very frightened	**Grammar** Uses of *to* + infinitive **Vocabulary** *-ed / -ing* adjectives		35
6C	What do you think I should do?	**Everyday English** Asking for and giving advice	**Pronunciation** Main stress	36
6D	I often worry about tests and exams	**Reading** An email asking for advice	**Writing skills** Linking: ordering ideas and giving examples **Writing** An email giving advice	37
Reading and listening extension		**Reading** A magazine advice column	**Listening** A conversation about problems with studying	38
Review and extension		WORDPOWER verb + *to*		39

Unit 7 Changes			Page
7A I'm the happiest I've ever been	**Grammar** Comparatives and superlatives **Vocabulary** *get* collocations		40
7B I didn't use to eat healthy food	**Grammar** *used to* **Vocabulary** Health collocations		41
7C It hurts all the time	**Everyday English** Doctors' questions	**Pronunciation** Tones for asking questions	42
7D After that, I decided to make a change	**Reading** A blog	**Writing skills** Linking: ordering events **Writing** A blog post about making changes	43
Reading and listening extension	**Reading** An article about how things were in the past	**Listening** A conversation about changes	44
Review and extension	**WORDPOWER** *change*		45
Unit 8 Culture			
8A My favourite book is based on a true story	**Grammar** The passive: present and past simple **Vocabulary** Art and music; Common verbs in the passive		46
8B I've hated rugby since I was at school	**Grammar** Present perfect with *for* and *since* **Vocabulary** Sports and activities	**Pronunciation** Word stress	47
8C I'm really sorry I haven't called	**Everyday English** Apologies and excuses	**Pronunciation** Tones for continuing or finishing	48
8D I couldn't put the book down	**Reading** A review of a famous book	**Writing skills** Positive and negative comments; Linking: *although*, *however* **Writing** A book review	49
Reading and listening extension	**Reading** An article from a tourist brochure	**Listening** A conversation about tourism in Australia	50
Review and extension	**WORDPOWER** *by*		51
Unit 9 Achievement			
9A If I don't pass this exam, I won't be very happy	**Grammar** First conditional **Vocabulary** Degree subjects; Education collocations	**Pronunciation** Word groups	52
9B I managed to stop feeling shy	**Grammar** Verb patterns **Vocabulary** Verbs followed by *to* + infinitive / verb + *-ing*		53
9C Who's calling, please?	**Everyday English** Telephoning people you know; Telephoning people you don't know	**Pronunciation** Main stress: contrastive	54
9D Online courses are new to me	**Reading** The profile of a French student	**Writing skills** Avoiding repetition **Writing** A student profile	55
Reading and listening extension	**Reading** An article about studying in the UK	**Listening** A conversation between a student and a professor	56
Review and extension	**WORDPOWER** Multi-word verbs with *put*		57
Unit 10 Values			
10A Would you do the right thing?	**Grammar** Second conditional **Vocabulary** Multi-word verbs	**Pronunciation** Sentence stress: vowel sounds	58
10B I'm too embarrassed to complain	**Grammar** Quantifiers; *too / not enough* **Vocabulary** Noun formation	**Pronunciation** Word stress	59
10C Can I exchange it for something else?	**Everyday English** Returning goods and making complaints	**Pronunciation** Sentence stress	60
10D We're really sorry we missed it	**Reading** Emails with apologies	**Writing skills** Formal and informal language **Writing** An email to apologise	61
Reading and listening extension	**Reading** An article about smartphones	**Listening** A conversation about online shopping	62
Review and extension	**WORDPOWER** Multi-word verbs with *on*		63
Unit 11 Discovery and Invention			
11A It's a robot that looks like a human	**Grammar** Defining relative clauses **Vocabulary** Compound nouns	**Pronunciation** Word stress: compound nouns	64
11B I think they discovered it by chance	**Grammar** Articles **Vocabulary** Adverbials: luck and chance	**Pronunciation** Stress in adverbials	65
11C It's straight ahead	**Everyday English** Asking for and giving directions in a building	**Pronunciation** Sound and spelling: /ɜː/ and /ɔː/	66
11D In my opinion, it's because of the Internet	**Reading** Opinions about important inventions	**Writing skills** Expressing results and reasons **Writing** A web post giving an opinion	67
Reading and listening extension	**Reading** An amazing story	**Listening** A conversation about a crime	68
Review and extension	**WORDPOWER** Preposition + noun		69
Unit 12 Characters			
12A I had always thought they were dangerous	**Grammar** Past perfect **Vocabulary** Animals	**Pronunciation** Sound and spelling: /ʌ/, /ɔː/ and /əʊ/	70
12B He said I was selfish!	**Grammar** Reported speech **Vocabulary** Personality adjectives	**Pronunciation** Word stress	71
12C I'm pretty sure it's Japanese	**Everyday English** Agreeing and disagreeing	**Pronunciation** Main stress: contrastive	72
12D About an hour later, the rain stopped	**Reading** A story about a helpful act	**Writing skills** Linkers: past time **Writing** A story about an accident and a rescue	73
Reading and listening extension	**Reading** An article about buying a zoo	**Listening** A conversation about a bad experience	74
Review and extension	**WORDPOWER** *age*		75
Vox pop video			76
Audioscripts			82
Answer key			87

1A Do you play any sports?

1 VOCABULARY Common adjectives

a Underline the correct words to complete the sentences.
1 The new building opposite the university is *rude* / *ugly* / *alright*. I hate it!
2 Our new teacher is always very *serious* / *silly* / *rude*. We work very hard in her lessons and she never smiles or laughs.
3 The cakes in the new baker's are *silly* / *serious* / *delicious*!
4 My brother's new girlfriend is *ugly* / *gorgeous* / *delicious*. I think she's a fashion model.
5 We played lots of *silly* / *horrible* / *perfect* games at Sarah's birthday party. I've got some really funny photos on Facebook.
6 Lily's a *perfect* / *strange* / *lovely* person. Her grandchildren love visiting her.

b Complete the sentences with the adjectives in the box.

| ~~boring~~ alright awful amazing |
| delicious rude strange perfect |

1 I'm not interested in football. It's so _boring_.
2 Thanks for the chocolates. They were _delicious_!
3 Look at this beautiful weather – it's a _perfect_ day to go to the beach.
4 The film we saw last night was really _strange_. I didn't understand it at all.
5 **A** How was the restaurant?
   B Oh, it was _awful_. There are better Italian restaurants in my town.
6 The weather in Scotland was _alright_. It rained every day.
7 The band were _amazing_! It was the best concert I've ever been to.
8 The waiter in the hotel was _rude_. He said we were stupid because we couldn't speak English very well!

2 GRAMMAR Question forms

a Underline the correct words to complete the questions.
1 How many children *he does have* / *does he have* / *does have he*?
2 Where *did you meet* / *did meet you* / *you met* your husband?
3 *Did he grow up* / *He grew up* / *He did grow up* in this area?
4 What *was like the film* / *was the film like* / *the film was like*?
5 How much *paid you* / *you did pay* / *did you pay* for your smartphone?
6 *Why she go* / *Why she went* / *Why did she go* to the USA?
7 How many films *he made* / *did he make* / *did make he* last year?
8 How *was your holiday* / *your holiday was* / *did your holiday be*?

b Put the words in the correct order to make questions.
1 you / Sarah's friend / are ?
   Are you Sarah's friend?
2 work / a bank / he / does / in ?
   Does he work in a bank?
3 you / last month / to New York / go / did / why ?
   Why did you go to New York last month?
4 like / that new Brazilian / what / restaurant / is ?
   What is that new Brazilian restaurant like?
5 with your sister / who / that man / was ?
   Who was that man with your sister?
6 TV programmes / you / do / watch / what type of ?
   What type of TV programmes do you watch?
7 go to / did / which university / you ?
   Which university did you go to?
8 did / how much / cost / the tickets ?
   How much did the ticket cost?

4

1B I'm really into Facebook

1 VOCABULARY Adverbs

a Put the words in brackets in the correct place in each sentence.

1 They see their grandchildren now that they live in Australia. (hardly ever)
   They hardly ever see their grandchildren now that they live in Australia.
2 I enjoy watching old Hollywood movies. (particularly)
   I particularly enjoy watching old Hollywood movies.
3 She hates it when people are late for meetings. (absolutely)
   She absolutely hates it when people are late for meetings.
4 We go to Italian restaurants, but sometimes we also go to Turkish ones. (generally)
   We generally go to Italian restaurants.
5 We're sure his flight arrives at Terminal 2, but I need to check it. (pretty)
   We're pretty sure his flight arrives at Terminal 2.
6 I hope she brings her gorgeous brother to the party! (really)
   I really hope she brings her gorgeous brother to the party.

b Underline the correct adverbs to complete the sentences.

1 I love rock music, but I absolutely / *especially* / fairly like The Rolling Stones. They're my favourite band.
2 He *hardly ever* / never / especially phones his mother – maybe once or twice a month.
3 I rarely / pretty / *normally* enjoy horror films, but this one was awful!
4 She's fairly / *absolutely* / rarely good-looking, but I don't think she's beautiful.
5 I never / *really* / hardly ever hate maths. I just don't understand it!
6 She generally / particularly / *rarely* takes her family out for dinner – only when it's her birthday.
7 They love all sports, but they're fairly / *mainly* / pretty interested in football. They watch all the matches on TV.
8 It's *pretty* / normally / rarely cold today, so why don't you take your gloves?

2 PRONUNCIATION Long and short vowels

a ▶1.1 Listen to the words. Do the letters in **bold** make long or short vowel sounds? Tick (✓) the words with long vowel sounds.

1 ✓ b**i**rthday — long
2 ☐ b**a**nk — short
3 ☐ c**i**nema — long
4 ☐ f**oo**d — short
5 ☐ p**a**rty — long
6 ☐ s**i**lly — short
7 ☐ m**u**sic — long
8 ☐ sp**o**rt — long
9 ☐ fr**ie**ndly — short
10 ☐ bl**o**g — short

3 GRAMMAR Present simple and present continuous

a Underline the correct verb forms to complete the sentences.

1 She is loving / *loves* / love reading fashion magazines at the hairdresser's.
2 We usually are going / goes / *go* to the café opposite the hotel.
3 I *'m reading* / read / reading a great book in English at the moment.
4 He 's wanting / does want / *wants* to phone his family in Tokyo. Can he use this phone?
5 Why *are you waiting* / do you wait / you waiting for the bus? Let's walk home.
6 I hardly ever am visiting / *visit* / visits my cousins in Ireland.
7 She studies / studying / *'s studying* French politics at university this term.
8 Yes, they're here. They play / *'re playing* / playing a computer game in the living room.

b Complete the conversation with the present simple or present continuous forms of the verbs in brackets. Use contractions where possible.

ALICE   What ¹ 's Sarah doing (Sarah, do) in that shop?
NAOMI   She ² is buying (buy) some postcards to send to her family.
ALICE   Really? I ³ don't generally ⁴ send (not send) postcards. I usually ⁵ write (write) a message on my Facebook wall. And sometimes I ⁶ put (put) a few photos of my holiday on my wall.
NAOMI   Yes, me too, but Sarah's grandparents ⁷ don't have (not have) a computer, so she ⁸ sends (send) them postcards instead.
ALICE   Oh, and what ⁹ are they (Tom and Jack, do) doing this morning?
NAOMI   They ¹⁰ spend (spend) the day at the beach.
ALICE   But Tom ¹¹ doesn't like (not like) swimming in the sea. He says the water's too cold.
NAOMI   Yes, but it ¹² is (be) really hot today!

c ▶1.2 Listen and check.

5

1C Everyday English
It was really nice to meet you

1 USEFUL LANGUAGE
Greeting people; Ending a conversation

a Underline the correct words to complete the conversation.

SAM   Hi, James! ¹*Much / Long / Very* time no see! How are you?
JAMES   Hi, Sam. I'm fine, thanks. ²*What a / What / How* lovely surprise! Great to see you!
SAM   Yes, it's really nice ³*see you / to see you / you see*, too.
JAMES   Where are you living ⁴*today / this day / these days*?
SAM   Oh, not ⁵*far from / far of / far away* here. In Park Road, near the sports centre.
JAMES   Oh, ⁶*what / how / who* nice!
SAM   And ⁷*she is / it is / this is* my wife, Jackie.
JAMES   Your wife – wow! That's fantastic ⁸*new / news / notices*! Nice to ⁹*meet / meat / meeting* you, Jackie.
JACKIE   Nice to meet you, ¹⁰*two / too / to*.

b ▶ 1.3 Listen and check.

c Complete the sentences with the words in the box.

surprise   hello   meet   news   again
time   last   ~~nice~~   must   up

1 Sea View Road? Oh, how __nice__!
2 Your husband – wow! That's fantastic __news__!
3 We really __must__ go. We're late.
4 What a lovely __surprise__!
5 Say __hello__ to Roger for me.
6 Long __time__ no see!
7 It was really nice to __see__ you.
8 We must meet __up__ soon.
9 It was great to see you __again__.
10 When did we __last__ see each other?

d ▶ 1.4 Listen and check.

2 PRONUNCIATION
Sentence stress

a ▶ 1.5 Listen to the sentences and underline the stressed words.

1 I'm <u>pretty</u> sure it was <u>two</u> <u>months</u> <u>ago</u>.
2 What a lovely surprise!
3 It was really nice to meet you.
4 I'm sorry, but I really must go.
5 Where are you living these days?
6 I'm late for a meeting.

1D Skills for Writing
I'm sending you some photos

1 READING

a Read Nandeep's email to Hannah and tick (✓) the correct answer.

   a ☐ Nandeep is staying at the Taj Mahal hotel in Delhi.
   b ☑ Nandeep is visiting his cousins in Boston.
   c ☐ Nandeep is on holiday at his aunt and uncle's house in Delhi.

b Read the email again. Are the sentences true or false?

   1 Nandeep mainly speaks in Hindi to his cousins. *false*
   2 He's visiting lots of places while he's in India. *yes*
   3 The Taj Mahal is in Delhi. *correct*
   4 Nandeep didn't enjoy visiting the Taj Mahal. *false*
   5 Nandeep often uses his aunt and uncle's pool. *yes*
   6 Nandeep isn't enjoying his holiday. *false*

Hi Hannah,

I hope you're enjoying your stay in Boston.

I'm spending a month on holiday in India. I'm staying with my aunt and uncle and my two cousins in Delhi. I don't speak much Hindi, but they all speak English very well, so communication isn't a problem. They're taking me to see lots of really interesting places. Yesterday we drove to Agra and visited the Taj Mahal. It took two hours to get there. This is a photo I took – what an amazing building!

It's really hot here all the time, but my aunt and uncle have a swimming pool, so we spend a lot of our time in the water – it's so relaxing! In the evenings I usually go to cafés with my cousins and their friends.

I'm having a great time here in India!

See you soon.

Nandeep

---

2 WRITING SKILLS
Correcting mistakes

a Correct the sentences.

   1 I'm having a lovely time here in france.
      <u>I'm having a lovely time here in France.</u>
   2 Yesterday we visitted the Palace of Versailles near Paris.
      <u>We visited the Palace of Versailles near Paris yesterday</u>
   3 In the mornings, I usually going to the beach with my Portuguese friends.
      <u>I usually go to the beach with my Portuguese friends in the morning.</u>
   4 I hope your having a lovely time in Canada with your family.
      _____
   5 Their English are very good, but we always speak in German.
      <u>Their english is very good but we always speak in German.</u>

3 WRITING

a Read the email from Paul. Use the notes in brackets to write Becky's reply.

◀ ✉

Hi Becky

Hope you're having a nice holiday.
Tell me all about it! (*Describe my holiday*)

What's the hotel like? (*Not in a hotel – staying with my family!*)

What do you do every day? (*Explain and send a photo*)

See you soon (*he OK? Ask.*)

Love
Paul

7

UNIT 1
Reading and listening extension

1 READING

a Read the article. Match the statements 1–3 with the people a–c.
1 I don't think internet dating is a good way to meet people. — a Joanna
2 Most people I've met online are friendly. — b Stephen
3 I'm very happy with the person I met online. — c Colm

INTERNET DATING:
How is it for you?

Are you looking for that special person? Do you want to meet new people? Lots of people meet their new partner over the Internet. It is particularly popular in the U.S.A., where about 30% of people meet their partner online. We talked to some young people in Ireland about their experiences of internet dating.

JOANNA, 23, CORK
I am dating a man I met on the Internet. His name is Gavin and he is lovely. We have the same hobbies and we laugh about the same things. We rarely argue and our relationship is perfect. I'm so happy.

STEPHEN, 28, DUBLIN
I normally wouldn't meet someone through the Internet. I prefer to meet people face-to-face. I think it's difficult to know what a person is like from a photo or some information online. I want to get to know someone properly, and I don't think you can do that on the Internet.

COLM, 22, GALWAY
I have several friends who I have met online. It's a great way to meet new people who have similar interests to you. Sometimes people can be rude but most people are very friendly – it's great fun! I recommend it as a good way of meeting new people.

There might be some problems with meeting people online, but lots of people are doing it these days, and it helps people meet new people and make new friends. Good luck!

b Read the article again and tick (✓) the best endings for the sentences.
1 In the U.S.A. …
   a ☐ people rarely use the Internet to find love.
   b ✓ internet dating is a normal way to meet people.
   c ☐ 30% of young people have a boyfriend or girlfriend.
2 Joanna …
   a ☐ has met several people online.
   b ✓ is very happy in her relationship.
   c ☐ doesn't think internet dating is right for her.
3 Stephen …
   a ☐ would like to meet a girl online.
   b ☐ doesn't want to put a photo of himself online.
   c ✓ doesn't think that you can get to know people online.
4 Colm thinks that …
   a ☐ it's difficult to meet people online.
   b ☐ people are often unfriendly.
   c ✓ the Internet is a good way to meet people and have fun.
5 The writer of the article thinks that …
   a ☐ people hardly ever meet someone they like online.
   b ✓ internet dating can be a good way to meet people.
   c ☐ internet dating is the best way to meet people.

c Write a paragraph about different ways of meeting new people. Think about:
- different places to meet new people
- some problems with meeting people for the first time
- the stories in the article
- your own experience.

During the Easter, I visited two churches. I introd[uced] with lots of different countries' people. For insta[nce] Italy, Hungarian, Malasian, Japanese, Chinese, England Saudy Arabian. When we met first time, we asked name's each other. After that where were they from what are they doing. How long are they living in Brit[ain] etc. When I meet other people I usually ask some place address and sometimes time.

… Review and extension

1 GRAMMAR

Correct the sentences.

1 Where you went on holiday last year?
   Where did you go on holiday last year?
2 At the moment, she works in the café by the station.
3 Why you missed the bus?
4 I can't talk to you now because I do my homework.
5 What kind of music you usually listen to?
6 They waiting for the bus to London.

Handwritten notes:
2. She is working in the cafe by the station at the moment.
3. Why do you miss the bus?
4. I can't talk to you now because I am doing my homework.

2 VOCABULARY

Correct the sentences.

1 The new Iron Man film is amaizing!
   The new Iron Man film is amazing!
2 We very enjoyed the film last night.
3 We had a lovly time at the party last night.
4 I think our History lessons are so borring.
5 I think that man's a bit extrange. Look, he's talking to himself.
6 New York's allright, but I prefer living in London, actually.

3 WORDPOWER *like*

Match 1–8 with a–h to make sentences.

1 [e] We can go for a walk in the park
2 [h] What was the party
3 [a] What gorgeous weather! It looks
4 [c] The boy in the white T-shirt looks
5 [g] He loves films with superheroes, you know,
6 [f] I absolutely love this singer. She sounds
7 [b] I want to buy a computer
8 [d] Thanks for your email. It sounds

a like the perfect day for the beach.
b like this one. How much is it?
c like Philip. They've got the same smile.
d like you're having a great holiday.
e if you like.
f like Katy Perry.
g like Batman or Spider-Man.
h like last night?

2 LISTENING

a ▶ 1.6 Listen to the conversation. Match 1–3 with a–c to make true sentences.

1 Sophia — a goes to a club every week.
2 Richard — b is friends with the people he lives with.
3 Peter — c meets people in a café every week.

b ▶ 1.6 Listen to the conversation again and tick (✓) the best endings for the sentences.

1 The radio programme is about …
   a ☐ starting university.
   b ☐ moving to a new city.
   c ✓ how people make friends.
2 Richard doesn't …
   a ✓ usually go to bars.
   b ☐ like making friends with new people.
   c ☐ find it difficult to meet people at university.
3 Richard likes …
   a ☐ going to parties with his friends.
   b ☐ people who like similar things to him.
   c ✓ the countryside near where he lives.
4 Sophia is interested in …
   a ☐ making friends with people studying Drama.
   b ☐ joining a club.
   c ✓ meeting lots of different people.
5 Peter doesn't …
   a ✓ use the Internet to meet people.
   b ☐ like the people he lives with.
   c ☐ usually go out in the evenings.
6 Which of the sentences is true about the students?
   a ✓ The university is helping all the students to make friends.
   b ☐ The students are making friends in different ways.

c Write questions and answers about what you do in your free time and who you spend it with.
Think about these questions:

- Where do you spend your free time?
- What do you do and how often?
- Who do you spend your free time with?

REVIEW YOUR PROGRESS

Look again at Review your progress on p.16 of the Student's Book. How well can you do these things now?
3 = very well   2 = well   1 = not so well

I CAN …

ask and answer personal questions	☐
talk about how I communicate	☐
greet people and end conversations	☐
write a personal email.	☐

9

2A We had an adventure

1 GRAMMAR Past simple

a Tick (✓) the correct sentences. Correct the wrong sentences.

1. ☐ The train not arrived until 22:30, so we got home around midnight.
   The train didn't arrive until 22:30, so we got home around midnight.
2. ☐ I slept very badly on the plane, so I feeled very tired the next day.
   _____
3. ☐ Did you took the train from New York to Washington?
   _____
4. ☐ We flew from London to Manchester because it was really cheap.
   _____
5. ☐ They spended two nights in a hotel and then they stayed at a friend's house for three days.
   _____
6. ☐ I didn't enjoyed my trip to Scotland because the weather wasn't very good.
   _____
7. ☐ When I got back to my hotel, I found a message from my sister.
   _____
8. ☐ We unpacked our suitcases and ate dinner in the hotel restaurant. It cost 100 euros!
   _____

b Complete the exchanges with the past simple form of the verbs in brackets. Use contractions where possible.

1. **A** How ___was___ (be) your flight?
   B Fine, thanks, but I _____ (not sleep) because the seats _____ (not be) comfortable.
2. **A** What _____ (you, do) last summer?
   B We _____ (not have) much money, so we _____ (decide) to stay in the UK.
3. **A** Where _____ (Ben, go) on holiday last year?
   B He _____ (go) to Canada.
4. **A** _____ (you, bring) back any souvenirs from Jamaica?
   B Yes, I _____. (do) I _____ (buy) some Blue Mountain coffee.
5. **A** _____ (you, meet) your French friends when you were in Paris?
   B Yes, we _____. (do) We _____ (meet) them for dinner one evening.
6. **A** _____ (you, visit) your cousins in Los Angeles?
   B No, we _____ (not have) time.

2 VOCABULARY Tourism

a Match 1–8 with a–h to make sentences.

1. [d] We decided to go to China on holiday, so we had to get
2. ☐ I'm really bored. Why don't we do
3. ☐ James decided to go away
4. ☐ Going to the Olympics is great, but you need to book
5. ☐ It's a good idea to buy
6. ☐ Come on! Let's unpack
7. ☐ My daughter didn't have much money so she stayed
8. ☐ On the day you leave, you need to check out of

a to Scotland for the weekend.
b our bags and go out for lunch.
c in hostels when she went travelling for a year.
d a visa from the embassy.
e some sightseeing this afternoon?
f your accommodation before you go.
g your hotel by 11 o'clock.
h souvenirs here – they're very expensive at the airport.

b Write the names of the holiday items under the pictures.

1 suntan lotion   2 _____   3 _____

4 _____   5 _____   6 _____

3 PRONUNCIATION -ed endings

a Tick (✓) the verbs that have an extra syllable when we add -ed.

Infinitive	+ -ed	Extra syllable?
depart	departed	✓
love	loved	
listen	listened	
hate	hated	
sound	sounded	
look	looked	
post	posted	
invite	invited	
enjoy	enjoyed	
like	liked	

b ▶ 2.1 Listen and check.

2B Everyone was waiting for me

1 VOCABULARY Travel collocations

a Complete the sentences with the correct forms of the verbs in the box.

> miss   take off   get to   change   give   land
> set off   board   hitchhike   travel around

When I was a student, my best friend and I ¹travelled around Europe for a month. We didn't want to travel by train, so we ²_____. Once, a lorry driver ³_____ us a lift from Paris to Cannes – over 900 kilometres!

She ⁴_____ from her house at six o'clock in the morning. However, she ⁵_____ the 06:30 train because there was a traffic jam in the town centre.

Our plane ⁶_____ from Beijing 45 minutes late, but we ⁷_____ in Sydney ten minutes early!

Our journey from London to Glasgow was terrible! We ⁸_____ our train in London at two o'clock, but then we ⁹_____ trains in Birmingham and also in Manchester. In the end, we ¹⁰_____ Glasgow just after midnight!

b Underline the correct words to complete the sentences.

1 **A** Why was there a big *strike* / *traffic jam* / *lift* on the motorway this morning?
   B Because there was a *crash* / *strike* / *queue* between two cars at 7:30.
2 **A** Why did you *lose* / *miss* / *delay* your train?
   B Well, my friend was driving us to the station, but her GPS wasn't working, so we *set off* / *broke down* / *got lost*. In the end, we bought a map!
3 **A** Why were there *traffic jams* / *long delays* / *long queues* to all the flights from Heathrow Airport today?
   B Because there was a pilots' *strike* / *turbulence* / *delay* yesterday, so lots of planes are at the wrong airport today.
4 There was *a turbulence* / *something wrong* / *a strike* with our coach, so we waited for two hours at the service station.
5 It took me over an hour to get my ticket because there was a long *delay* / *queue* / *crash* at the ticket office. Then the train *got lost* / *took off* / *broke down* just outside Paris, so that's why I'm so late.
6 **A** It sounds like you had a bad flight between Washington and London.
   B Yes, there was a lot of *turbulence* / *queues* / *strikes* over the Atlantic because of the bad weather.

2 GRAMMAR Past continuous

a Complete the sentences with the past continuous forms of the verbs in brackets.

1 When we arrived at the station, my uncle _was waiting_ (wait) for us in the car park.
2 It _____ (snow) hard when we got to our hotel.
3 _____ (you, fly) over the Alps when the turbulence started?
4 How fast _____ (you, drive) when the accident happened?
5 Where _____ (you, stand) when the thief stole your handbag?
6 Did you get lost because your GPS _____ (not work)?

b Complete the text with the past simple or past continuous forms of the verbs in brackets.

My mother and I ¹ _had_ (have) a terrible journey from London to Edinburgh last weekend. First, when my brother ² _____ (drive) us to the airport on Saturday evening, his car ³ _____ (break down) on the motorway. In the end, we ⁴ _____ (miss) our plane and ⁵ _____ (buy) some new tickets for the flight on Sunday morning instead. However, on Sunday morning we ⁶ _____ (wait) for our flight when it ⁷ _____ (start) snowing heavily, and they ⁸ _____ (decide) to close the airport. So we ⁹ _____ (take) a taxi to Euston Station and ¹⁰ _____ (buy) tickets for the 2 pm train to Edinburgh.

3 PRONUNCIATION
Sentence stress: vowel sounds

a ▶2.2 Listen to the sentences. Do the letters in **bold** sound like /ə/ as in *computer*, /ɒ/ as in *dog* or /ɜː/ as in *her*? Tick (✓) the correct box for each sentence.

	Sound 1 /ə/ (e.g. comput**er**)	Sound 2 /ɒ/ (e.g. d**o**g)	Sound 3 /ɜː/ (e.g. h**er**)
1 W**e**re you waiting for the bus?	✓		
2 I w**a**sn't driving the car.			
3 They w**e**re watching TV.			
4 We w**e**ren't having dinner.			
5 She w**a**s talking on her phone.			
6 W**a**s she listening?			
7 He w**a**sn't smoking.			
8 They w**e**ren't playing chess.			

2C Everyday English
What time's the next train?

1 USEFUL LANGUAGE
Asking for information in a public place

a Put the words in the correct order to make questions.
1 anything else / help you / with / I / there / is / can ?
   Is there anything else I can help you with?
2 is / tell / where / information desk / you / me / the / could ?
   _____
3 Edinburgh / to / much / is / a return ticket / how ?
   _____
4 for the airport / leave / do / often / buses / how / the ?
   _____
5 Barcelona / time / the next coach / what / to / is ?
   _____
6 my ticket / pay / euros / can / for / in / I ?
   _____
7 can / a sandwich / the journey / for / where / buy / I ?
   _____
8 a taxi / to the airport / much / it / does / cost / to get / how ?
   _____

b ▶2.3 Listen and check.

c Complete the conversation with the words in the box.

| can | near here | have | over there | could you | ~~excuse~~ |
| anything else | actually | from | what time |

A ¹ _Excuse_ me.
B Yes, how ² _____ I help you?
A ³ _____ tell me which platform the next train to London leaves ⁴ _____ ?
B Certainly, madam: It leaves from Platform 2.
A OK, thanks. And ⁵ _____ does it leave?
B It leaves at 10:32, in twelve minutes.
A Brilliant. Thanks.
B Is there ⁶ _____ I can help you with?
A ⁷ _____, there is one more thing. Where can I buy a cup of coffee? Is there a café ⁸ _____ ?
B Yes, there is. There's a café on the platform, ⁹ _____.
A Great. Thanks so much.
B No problem. ¹⁰ _____ a good journey.

d ▶2.4 Listen and check.

e Match the traveller's sentences 1–8 with the ticket seller's responses a–h.
1 [c] Hello.
2 [ ] Could you tell me what time the next bus to Folkestone leaves, please?
3 [ ] Great, thanks! And where does it leave from?
4 [ ] I will be. Can I have a ticket, please?
5 [ ] Here you are. Also, is there somewhere I can buy a newspaper?
6 [ ] That's OK. I can run fast.
7 [ ] Yes, I think that's it. Thank you for your help!
8 [ ] Thanks! Bye!

a Goodbye!
b Yes, of course. It leaves in five minutes.
c Good afternoon. How can I help you?
d Certainly. That'll be £9.50.
e No problem, sir. Now hurry, or you'll miss your bus!
f From stop number 4, but you'll need to be quick!
g You'll need to! Is that all, sir?
h Yes, at the newsagent over there, but I'm not sure you'll have time.

2 PRONUNCIATION Joining words

a ▶2.5 Listen to the questions. Tick (✓) the two words that are joined together.
1 When did you check into your hotel?
   a [✓] che**ck i**nto   b [ ] you**r h**otel
2 How can I help you?
   a [ ] ca**n I**   b [ ] hel**p y**ou
3 Did you get a visa when you went to China?
   a [ ] ge**t a**   b [ ] whe**n y**ou
4 What time did you set off from home?
   a [ ] di**d y**ou   b [ ] se**t o**ff
5 What time is your plane?
   a [ ] ti**me i**s   b [ ] i**s y**our
6 How much is a return ticket to Bath?
   a [ ] mu**ch i**s   b [ ] to **B**ath

12

2D Skills for Writing
This city is different, but very friendly

1 READING

a Read Roberto's blog and tick (✓) the correct answers.

1 Roberto and Ana are staying in …
   a ☐ a hotel in the centre of London.
   b ☐ a hostel near Heathrow Airport.
   c ☐ a hotel in Earl's Court.
   d ☐ a hostel near the centre of London.

2 On Sunday, Roberto and Ana …
   a ☐ had fish and chips for lunch.
   b ☐ spent all day at the British Museum.
   c ☐ went to the British Museum and Covent Garden.
   d ☐ thought the British Museum was boring.

SATURDAY
Ana and I got to London at 11:30 this morning. It was a very long flight from São Paulo. When we got off the plane, the first thing we noticed was the cold – six degrees! I'm glad I brought a warm coat! In São Paulo, it was 35 degrees when we left. Everything they say about Londoners is true! The people at the airport weren't very friendly and they couldn't understand our English. And we couldn't understand what they were saying. In the end, we took the underground from Heathrow Airport to our hostel in Earl's Court, near the centre of London. The hostel is full of young tourists from all over the world and everyone was very friendly and helpful. We were very tired, so we decided to sleep for a few hours. Ana's telling me to get ready to go and eat, so I have to finish now – more tomorrow.

SUNDAY
Ana and I had our first experience of British food last night. We went to a little café near the hostel. We decided to try fish and chips. It's a typical British dish and it was delicious with a hot cup of tea (with milk!). Today we visited the British Museum and Covent Garden. The British Museum is amazing – there are lots of interesting things to see. We spent two hours there and only saw a few of the rooms. We bought some sandwiches for lunch and then we went to Covent Garden market. There were lots of musicians and magicians in the street. We had a lovely afternoon and Ana took lots of photos. You can see them on Facebook.

b Read the blog again. Are the sentences true or false?

1 On Saturday, it was warmer in London than in São Paulo.
2 It was difficult for Roberto and Ana to understand the people at the airport.
3 When they got to the hostel, they went to bed.
4 They didn't enjoy their fish and chips.
5 They didn't see all the rooms in the British Museum.
6 They had lunch in a restaurant in Covent Garden.

2 WRITING SKILLS Linking words

a <u>Underline</u> the correct words to complete the sentences.

1 There was a long queue for the museum, and / <u>so</u> / but we decided to go to the market instead.
2 We didn't visit the Tower of London because / so / but the tickets were very expensive.
3 The hotel looked really nice, because / and / but they didn't have any free rooms that night.
4 Yesterday I visited Ellis Island so / and / because the Statue of Liberty.
5 There weren't any flights today but / so / because there was a snow storm.
6 Because / When / So we got to our hotel, I phoned my wife to wish her 'Happy Birthday'.
7 It started raining hard, but / because / so we didn't go to the mountains.
8 We wanted to go to the concert, but / so / because we couldn't get any tickets.

3 WRITING

a Read the notes. Write Maite's blog post about her holiday in New York.

Maite's blog: New York post (notes)

Monday, 25th January

Madrid: left 12:20
New York: arrived 14:30
Very tired – (why?)
Weather: very cold – minus 6 degrees!
People = (?)
Hotel = (?)
Dinner = (?)

13

UNIT 2
Reading and listening extension

1 READING

a Read the article. How did the couples travel? Tick (✓) the correct ways. Sometimes there is more than one possible answer.

1 Carl and Sam
   a ☐ on foot
   b ✓ on two wheels
   c ✓ on four wheels
   d ☐ by sea
2 Ashish and Bryony
   a ☐ on foot
   b ☐ on two wheels
   c ☐ on four wheels
   d ☐ by sea
3 Yvette and Rob
   a ☐ on foot
   b ☐ on two wheels
   c ☐ on four wheels
   d ☐ by sea

b Read the article again and underline the correct words to complete the sentences.
1 Carl and Sam / Ashish and Bryony / <u>Yvette and Rob</u> stayed in Bristol for most of the week.
2 Carl and Sam / Ashish and Bryony / Yvette and Rob enjoyed the first day of the race.
3 Carl and Sam / Ashish and Bryony / Yvette and Rob stopped when they didn't know where they were.
4 Carl and Sam / Ashish and Bryony / Yvette and Rob finished their journey on foot when something happened to the vehicle they were in.
5 Carl and Sam / Ashish and Bryony / Yvette and Rob stopped after the first day.

c Complete the words to make sentences about the article. Write one word in each space.
1 During the race, the students c_ouldn't_ spend any money.
2 When they started the race, the weather was s_____.
3 Carl and Sam got a l_____ home with Carl's dad.
4 It c_____ money for Ashish and Bryony to stay in a hotel.
5 Yvette and Rob got to Spain early in the m_____.

d Write about a long journey you went on. Remember to include:
• where you went
• a description of how you travelled there
• what you thought of the place.

In July, a group of students from Bristol University, in England, had a race. It started at the university at 9 am on 20 June. The winners were the pair who travelled the longest distance in seven days without spending any money.

CARL AND SAM

We decided to cycle. The sun was shining when we set off and it was fun. But on the third day, it started raining and we got lost. It was awful. We slept under a tree in a field. The next morning Carl phoned his dad and he came to get us and drove us home.

DISTANCE TRAVELLED: 110 MILES

ASHISH AND BRYONY

We hitchhiked. A lorry stopped and we got in. There were long delays and we didn't go far for hours. That evening as we were driving north the lorry broke down and we had to get out. We didn't know what to do. We were tired and hungry so we decided to walk to a village and stay in a hotel. But we had to pay. The next day we went home.

DISTANCE TRAVELLED: 130 MILES

YVETTE AND ROB

We decided to walk to the port in Bristol and try to board a ship. We went to the office and asked if any ships would take us for free. For five days no one would. On the sixth day we found a ship to take us to Spain. We boarded the ship and the next day we arrived in Bilbao as the sun was rising. It was amazing.

DISTANCE TRAVELLED: 640 MILES

2 LISTENING

a ▶2.6 Listen to the conversation. Match problems a–e with where they are happening 1–5.

1 M3 — a crash and delays
2 M4 — b long delays
3 M1 — c no delays
4 Trains — d problems this weekend
5 Gatwick — e traffic jam

b ▶2.6 Listen to the conversation again and tick (✓) the correct answers.

1 Why were there delays on the M3 this morning?
 a ✓ There was a crash.
 b ☐ The police closed the road.
 c ☐ It was raining.
2 What happened three hours ago near Swindon?
 a ☐ There was an accident.
 b ☐ There was a very long queue.
 c ☐ A lorry stopped working.
3 Who should use the A429 this evening?
 a ☐ People who are going to Swindon.
 b ☐ Lorries.
 c ☐ Everyone on the M4.
4 Who did the police say can't go on the motorway?
 a ☐ People going to a music festival.
 b ☐ Hitchhikers.
 c ☐ People who want to camp.
5 What is unusual about the trains today?
 a ☐ There aren't any trains working.
 b ☐ The trains are mainly working well.
 c ☐ There are lots of delays.
6 Where did Jackie and Bob stay last night?
 a ☐ In a hotel at the airport.
 b ☐ On the floor at the airport.
 c ☐ In India.

c Write about a long journey you took. Remember to include:
- how you travelled
- how long it took
- what problems you had.

Review and extension

1 GRAMMAR

Correct the sentences.

1 When I did some housework, I heard the news on the radio.
 When I was doing some housework, I heard the news on the radio.
2 When we were getting to the station, the train was just arriving.
3 My wife phoned me while I waited for my plane.
4 A man was taking my wallet while I was waiting in the queue for my ticket.
5 Last year, we were going on holiday to Greece for two weeks.
6 I was driving to the airport when I was seeing the accident.

2 VOCABULARY

Correct the sentences.

1 They missed their flight because Rob's car broke on the way to the airport.
 They missed their flight because Rob's car broke down on the way to the airport.
2 My travel from Berlin to London took fifteen hours.
3 Last week, I went to Rome on a business travel.
4 The trafic was terrible because it was the rush hour.
5 By the time they checked away the hotel, it was 2 pm.
6 In the afternoon, they went sighseeing in the old town.

3 WORDPOWER off

Complete the sentences with the words in the box.

| 75% | I'm | set | ~~switched~~ | drove | took | are | fell |

1 He was tired when he went to bed, so he _switched_ off the light and went to sleep.
2 They _____ off from Paul's house at 3:00 and arrived in Paris at 11:30.
3 When I got to the hotel, I _____ off my shoes.
4 She _____ off her motorbike and broke her arm.
5 Those jeans are cheap! They're _____ off the original price.
6 He got in his car and _____ off without speaking.
7 Goodnight. _____ off now. I'm meeting a friend.
8 Ladies and gentlemen: the film is about to start, so please make sure your phones _____ off.

REVIEW YOUR PROGRESS

Look again at Review your progress on p.26 of the Student's Book. How well can you do these things now?
3 = very well 2 = well 1 = not so well

I CAN ...

talk about past holidays	☐
describe difficult journeys	☐
ask for information in a public place	☐
write a travel blog.	☐

3A Have you ever helped a stranger?

1 GRAMMAR
Present perfect or past simple

a Put the words in the correct order to make sentences.
1. has / that old lady's / done / shopping / James / lots of times .
   James has done that old lady's shopping lots of times.
2. you / have / to / been / in / Rio de Janeiro / carnival / the / ever ?
   _____
3. twice this week / I / to charity / money / given / have .
   _____
4. have / you / my / with / helped / homework / me / never .
   _____
5. they / volunteer work / ever / done / have / any ?
   _____
6. big / never / a / for the waiter / left / tip / has / she .
   _____
7. money / have / any / you / homeless person / to / given / ever / a ?
   _____
8. several times / I / visited / this month / my / have / grandmother .
   _____

b Complete the exchanges with the present perfect or past simple forms of the words in brackets.
1. **A** *Have you ever given* money to charity? (you, ever, give)
   B Yes, I _____ £10 to a cancer charity last week. (give)
2. **A** _____ volunteer work in Africa before? (she, ever, do)
   B Yes, she _____ some volunteer work in Mali last year. (do)
3. **A** _____ someone who was hurt? (you, ever, help)
   B Yes, I _____ a woman who fell off her bike last week. (help)
4. **A** I _____ tips in that restaurant lots of times. (leave)
   B Really? How much _____ the last time you came? (you, leave)
5. **A** _____ drinks for 20 people? (he, ever, buy)
   B Yes, he _____ a drink for all his friends on his birthday in July. (buy)

2 VOCABULARY
make / do / give collocations

a Match 1–8 with a–h to make sentences.
1. [d] She was a very confident girl, so she made
2. [ ] When she read the email from her nephew, it made
3. [ ] Are you doing anything
4. [ ] He's a really funny guy. He always makes
5. [ ] Your daughter's very clever. Is she doing
6. [ ] My grandfather always gives us
7. [ ] We gave the American tourists
8. [ ] He didn't use his camera any more, so he gave it

a away to his grandson.
b silly jokes when he's with friends.
c a big hug when we go to see him.
d lots of friends at her new school.
e nice for your birthday?
f directions to the train station.
g well at school this term?
h her smile because it was so funny.

b Underline the correct words to complete the sentences.
1. I love those old black-and-white films. Charlie Chaplin always *does* / *makes* / *gives* me smile.
2. You're so mean. You never *do* / *make* / *give* the waiters a tip.
3. He *made* / *did* / *gave* volunteer work for a charity in Africa last year.
4. She was so happy to see him again that she *gave* / *made* / *did* him a big hug.
5. Do your parents usually *make* / *give* / *do* something nice when it's their wedding anniversary?
6. I'm having a great time in Paris. I've *made* / *done* / *given* some new friends in the hostel.
7. The doctors say that she's *making* / *giving* / *doing* well and that she can leave the hospital tomorrow.
8. I've never *made* / *given* / *done* anyone directions in French – all the tourists who come here speak English.

3B I've already spent my salary this month

1 VOCABULARY Money

a Match 1–8 with a–h to make sentences.

1. [f] My company pays my salary
2. [ ] That holiday sounds fantastic, but
3. [ ] My brother lent me £50 yesterday
4. [ ] If you can't afford to buy a new car,
5. [ ] She's just spent £150
6. [ ] I only buy clothes from that shop
7. [ ] If you buy two jackets,
8. [ ] When I borrow money

a so I could buy some new jeans.
b from my parents, I always pay it back quickly.
c when they have special offers.
d we can give you a 20% discount.
e on two pairs of shoes.
f into my bank account.
g it costs £5,000 just for a week!
h why don't you get a loan from the bank?

b Complete the text with the words in the box.

> into afford lend spend bank account
> up for borrow back loan

I'm saving ¹ _up for_ a car at the moment. I pay £200 ² _____ my ³ _____ each month. I can't ⁴ _____ to buy a new car, so it will have to be second-hand – probably three or four years old. My parents have offered to ⁵ _____ me some money but I don't want to ⁶ _____ any money from them. They've just bought a very old house in the country and they need to ⁷ _____ a lot of money on repairs. So I'm going to ask the bank for a ⁸ _____ of £5,000. I think I can pay it ⁹ _____ in two years.

2 GRAMMAR Present perfect with just, already and yet

a Underline the correct adverbs to complete the sentences.

1. I've *just / already / yet* spent £100 this weekend, so I'm afraid I can't afford to go to a restaurant for dinner.
2. It's Mum's birthday tomorrow – have you bought her a present *already / just / yet*?
3. Look, I've *just / already / yet* bought a new mobile phone. It's brilliant, isn't it?
4. He's *yet / just / already* saved up £3,000 because he wants to travel round the world next summer.
5. **A** Why does she look so upset?
   B Because she's *already / just / yet* lost her wallet.
6. No, I can't lend you any more money. You've *already / just / yet* borrowed £100 from me.
7. Oh, no! We can't play tennis now because it's *already / yet / just* started raining.
8. She hasn't opened a new bank account *already / yet / just*.

b Correct the sentences.

1. Mike just has spent £400 on a new camera.
   Mike has just spent £400 on a new camera.
2. He's borrowed already £2,000 from his bank.
   _____
3. Have you yet paid Louise back?
   _____
4. Sue already has spent the money she borrowed from me.
   _____
5. We've bought just a new TV in the sales.
   _____
6. Has she saved yet enough money to buy a tablet?
   _____
7. I've bought already a present for my wife.
   _____
8. They've opened a new bank account in France just.
   _____

17

3C Everyday English
Do you have anything cheaper?

1 USEFUL LANGUAGE
Talking to people in shops

a Put the conversation in the correct order.

- [ ] **B** Yes, I suppose she might like them. On second thoughts, maybe I should get something else.
- [1] **A** Good morning. Can I help you?
- [ ] **B** Do you have anything cheaper?
- [ ] **A** OK. Er, let me see ... what about this necklace?
- [ ] **B** Yes, it's lovely. OK, I'll take it.
- [ ] **A** Are you looking for anything in particular?
- [ ] **B** Er, yes. I'm looking for a present for my wife.
- [ ] **A** Really? How about these earrings? They're really beautiful. A perfect present ...
- [ ] **B** Well, she loves earrings.
- [ ] **A** Well, these earrings here are cheaper. They're only £50 with the discount.

b ▶3.1 Listen and check.

c Underline the correct words to complete the sentences.
1. How would you like to *cost / pay / buy*?
2. We're looking *for / at / after* a present for my grandfather.
3. Did you want something *on / in / at* particular?
4. Who's *then / after / next*, please?
5. *In second thoughts / On second thoughts / My second thought*, I really think we should get her a book.
6. Can you *enter / write / touch* your PIN, please?
7. Do you have this in a different *size / till / receipt*? Thanks.
8. Could you show us *something more / something else / something other*?

d Put the words in the correct order to make sentences.
1. for / jacket / looking / a / I'm .
   I'm looking for a jacket.
2. a / 14 / size / I'm / I / think .
   _____
3. same / in / have / one / blue / do / the / you ?
   _____
4. much / tell / can / it / how / is / you / me ?
   _____
5. a bit / too / that's / expensive .
   _____
6. one / you / cheaper / do / have / a ?
   _____

2 PRONUNCIATION Sentence stress

a ▶3.2 Listen to the sentences and underline the stressed syllables or words.
1. Can you <u>show</u> us something <u>else</u>?
2. Can you enter your PIN, please?
3. I'm looking for a present for my husband.
4. Do you have any black jeans?
5. Thanks. I'll take it.
6. Actually, I think we should buy her a book.

3D Skills for Writing
We've successfully raised £500

1 READING

a Read David and Philip's email and tick (✓) the correct answer.

David and Philip are writing to …
- a ☐ ask their colleagues for more money.
- b ☐ invite their colleagues to a party.
- c ☐ tell their colleagues about Cancer Research and how they have all helped.
- d ☐ ask their colleagues to swim a kilometre.

b Read David and Philip's email again. Are the sentences true or false?

1. In the last year they have given £2,500 to Cancer Research.
2. In April, 30 people swam a kilometre to raise money.
3. The party in June was very popular.
4. 4,000 people with cancer get money from Cancer Research.

2 WRITING SKILLS Paragraphing

a Read the sentences. Put them in the correct order to make an email with four paragraphs. The paragraphs should be in the following order:
- Introduction
- How the team has raised / raises money
- Information about ActionAid
- Closing the email

☐ Thanks again for all your help. Please look out for our next event.
☐ ActionAid will use the money to help poor people around the world, to educate them and to protect them. In the past ten years, they have helped thousands of children start school.
☐ We have successfully raised £750.
☐ And, of course, next Friday there is the book and DVD sale at lunchtime.
☐ 1 We'd like to thank everyone for helping to raise money for ActionAid over the past year.
☐ Most of you came to the 1970s party in September. A lot of people also came to our karaoke night in November.
☐ So remember that a small amount of money can make a big difference. For example, only £4 per week gives a child in Africa clean water, education and medicine.

✉ Mail

Hello everyone,

We'd like to say a big 'Thank you!' to everyone who has helped us to raise money for Cancer Research over the past six months. We've successfully raised £2,500!

We really hope you have enjoyed the various events that we have organised this year. First we had a 'Swimathon' in April. Thirty of us swam a kilometre and raised over £1,000. Then 200 people came to our fantastic summer party in June. And don't forget to come to our special quiz night in September. There are some amazing prizes!

Cancer Research will use the money to do important research. This includes the work of over 4,000 scientists, doctors and nurses who are fighting cancer in this country. Cancer Research helps thousands of people with cancer every year.

Would you like to help us raise more money for Cancer Research? Please look out for the next event. Thanks again for all your help.

David and Philip

3 WRITING

a Read the notes and write Sam's email to his colleagues about the Save the Children charity.

Email to colleagues about Save the Children

Introduction:
Thank you – everyone who helped raise money – past 12 months. How much?

How the team has raised money and future events:
September: sports day
October: 1990s karaoke evening
Next week: quiz night + prizes!

Information about Save the Children:
Our money = save children's lives + better future
Last year STC helped 10m children around world
Small amount of money = big difference, e.g. £3 saves lives of 8 children with stomach virus

Closing the email
Help raise more money for STC?
Email me for info about future events
Thanks again

UNIT 3
Reading and listening extension

1 READING

a Read the magazine article. Complete the sentences with the numbers in the box.

| 100   10 million   13 million   ~~87 million~~ |

1 A company bought the website for £ _87 million_.
2 He started the website with £_____.
3 The website has more than _____ regular users.
4 Charities got £_____ from Martin after he sold the website.

MARTIN LEWIS: THE MONEY MAN

Martin Lewis is a British journalist, TV presenter and writer. He knows a lot about money: how to spend it, where to use it, and, most of all, how to save it!

Martin was always interested in saving money and helping other people to save money. He gave tips to friends about it, he talked about it on television and he wrote about it in a national newspaper. In 2003, he decided to start a website, *moneysavingexpert.com*. He paid a man in Uzbekistan £100 to design the site and soon thousands of people were using it. The website gave lots of useful information. It told people which times of the day supermarkets had the most special offers. It helped people get discounts on everything from clothes to holidays. It told people when shops had sales on. The website helped people to buy things that they couldn't afford to buy before. And if you needed to borrow money to buy a new car or a house, it told you which banks were the best to lend it to you. Lots of people started using *moneysavingexpert.com* and started telling their friends about it.

The website has been a huge success and Martin has done very well. Over 13 million people now use *moneysavingexpert.com* every month and in 2012, Martin Lewis sold the site to another company for £87 million. But Martin hasn't stopped helping people. Since selling the website, he has given away over £10 million to charities that help people look after their money. He's certainly made a lot of people smile. And it all started with £100.

b Read the magazine article again. Are the sentences true or false?

1 Martin Lewis is an expert on how to spend less money.
2 It took a long time before anyone used the website.
3 People can save money by going to supermarkets at a particular time of the day.
4 Martin Lewis still owns the website.
5 *Moneysavingexpert.com* has made Martin a very rich man.

c Complete the summary of the magazine article with the correct forms of the verbs in the box.

| borrow   buy   call   cost   get
  save   spend   ~~work~~   write |

Before 2003, Martin Lewis ¹ _worked_ as a journalist and ² _____ about how to save money. In 2003, it ³ _____ him £100 to start a website, which he ⁴ _____ *moneysavingexpert.com*. It was soon very popular. It has lots of information about how to ⁵ _____ less money in shops, how to open a bank account, how to ⁶ _____ a discount on products and where to ⁷ _____ money from. The website has helped millions of people to ⁸ _____ money or get a loan since 2003. A company ⁹ _____ the website in 2012 for £87 million.

c Write about something that you have borrowed from or lent to someone. Include answers to these questions:
- What was it?
- Who did you lend it to or borrow it from?
- How long for?

2 LISTENING

a ▶3.3 Listen to the conversation. Underline the correct people to complete the sentences.

1 *Anita / Gary / Mike* gave a man something that he didn't have.
2 *Anita / Gary / Mike* is helping a friend who doesn't have much money.
3 *Anita / Gary / Mike* does something nice for other people every week.
4 *Anita / Gary / Mike* asked other people to lend her things.
5 *Anita / Gary / Mike* made friends with the person he helped.

b **3.3** Listen to the conversation again and tick (✓) the correct answers.

1 Why is Anita's neighbour having a party?
  a ✓ It's her daughter's birthday.
  b ☐ It's her son's birthday.
  c ☐ It's her husband's birthday.
2 Where is the birthday party going to be?
  a ☐ At the local beach.
  b ☐ In the back garden.
  c ☐ In the local park.
3 What did the Greek man do?
  a ☐ He borrowed an umbrella from Gary.
  b ☐ He lent an umbrella to Gary.
  c ☐ He borrowed Gary's coat.
4 What happened when Gary saw the man again?
  a ☐ They had lunch.
  b ☐ They had a cup of tea.
  c ☐ They went on holiday together.
5 What has Gary just bought?
  a ☐ A ticket to the theatre.
  b ☐ A ticket to Adelaide.
  c ☐ A ticket to Greece.
6 How does Mike try and make people smile?
  a ☐ He gives them money.
  b ☐ He puts his arms around them.
  c ☐ He makes friends with them.

c Write about the nicest thing that you've ever done. Remember to include:
 • who you helped
 • why you helped them
 • what you did
 • how they felt and how you felt afterwards.

Review and extension

1 GRAMMAR

Correct the sentences.
1 I never left a big tip in a restaurant.
  I've never left a big tip in a restaurant.
2 Did you ever give money to charity?
3 I've been to China on business last year.
4 I just bought a new mobile phone.
5 I haven't bought yet a birthday present for my brother.
6 I already spent £200 this weekend.

2 VOCABULARY

Correct the sentences.
1 I've just opened an account bank in the UK.
  I've just opened a bank account in the UK.
2 Can you borrow me 50 euros, please?
3 Joe did a really funny joke, but nobody laughed.
4 James is saving on for a new computer.
5 Our taxi driver was very friendly, so we made him a big tip.
6 I bought a new laptop in the sells – it was only £150!
7 Have you ever made any volunteer work?
8 Tony owes to me £50, but he hasn't paid it back yet.

3 WORDPOWER just

Complete the sentences with the words in the box.

about spoken in time like ~~coming~~
a beginner over under

1 I'm just _coming_. I'll be there in two minutes!
2 There was a lot of traffic but we got to the airport just _____ for our flight.
3 My watch cost just _____ €100. Not cheap at all!
4 You're just _____ your mother – you have the same blue eyes!
5 Dinner is just _____ ready. It'll be five minutes.
6 The film is 125 minutes long. It's just _____ two hours.
7 I've just _____ to him. He'll meet us at 9.00.
8 No, she can't give a presentation in English yet. She's just _____.

REVIEW YOUR PROGRESS

Look again at Review your progress on p.36 of the Student's Book. How well can you do these things now?
3 = very well   2 = well   1 = not so well

I CAN ...

talk about experiences of generosity	☐
talk about spending and saving money	☐
talk to people in shops	☐
write an update email.	☐

4A I'm going to the hairdresser's tomorrow

1 VOCABULARY
Clothes and appearance

a Match the pictures with the words in the box.

underwear tights sweatshirt tie high heels
tracksuit ~~gloves~~ sandals earrings jumper
flat shoes bracelet

1 _gloves_   2 _____   3 _____
4 _____   5 _____   6 _____
7 _____   8 _____   9 _____
10 _____   11 _____   12 _____

b Complete the conversation with the present continuous forms of the verbs in the box. Use contractions where possible.

stay come bring not fly ~~arrive~~ take meet (x2)

A So what have you arranged for this evening?
B Well, my parents ¹ _are arriving_ at the station on the 6:30 train from Paris.
A So, ² _____ you ³ _____ them at the station?
B Yes, we are. We ⁴ _____ a taxi from our house at 6:00. I booked it this morning.
A Good. So where ⁵ _____ they ⁶ _____?
B At the Hilton Hotel. They've got a double room with a balcony.
A Great. And what about the restaurant?
B I've reserved a table for eight at eight o'clock. Everyone ⁷ _____ to the restaurant at 7:45 so we can all be there when they arrive.
A Brilliant. Have you told the restaurant that it's your father's birthday?
B Yes, they've made him a special cake with HAPPY 60TH on it. They ⁸ _____ it to our table at ten o'clock, together with the coffee.
A And what about tomorrow?
B They ⁹ _____ to Scotland until the afternoon, so there's plenty of time. Their flight's at 3:30.
A Great, so it's all arranged. I have to go now because I ¹⁰ _____ Sally for a coffee in ten minutes. See you later!

c ▶4.1 Listen and check.

2 GRAMMAR
Present continuous and *going to*

a Put the words in the correct order to make sentences.
1 buy / going / a new dress / I'm / the party / for / to .
   I'm going to buy a new dress for the party.
2 going / your wedding / you / are / invite / your / to / cousin / to ?
   _____
3 aren't / going / they / get married / to / this / year .
   _____
4 going / are / do / after university / you / what / to ?
   _____
5 visit / Spain next year / going / we're / in / my relatives / to .
   _____
6 to / you / are / wear / to / the party / what / going ?
   _____

3 PRONUNCIATION
Sound and spelling: *going to*

a ▶4.2 Listen to *going to* in the sentences. Do you hear /ˈɡəʊɪŋ tə/ (*going to*) or /ˈɡənə/ (*gonna*)? Tick (✓) the correct box for each sentence.

	/ˈɡəʊɪŋ tə/	/ˈɡənə/
1 Are you going to go out tonight?	☐	✓
2 What are you going to do for your birthday?	☐	☐
3 He isn't going to have a holiday this year.	☐	☐
4 We're going to try to find a taxi.	☐	☐
5 I'm going to have a shower after breakfast.	☐	☐
6 They aren't going to do their homework.	☐	☐
7 She's going to phone her brother.	☐	☐
8 I'm not going to go to Ibiza this year.	☐	☐

4B Shall we go to the market?

1 GRAMMAR will / won't / shall

a Match 1–8 with a–h to make sentences.

1. [c] Let's go on holiday to Greece next summer.
2. [ ] You know I don't really like hot food.
3. [ ] Which film shall we see with the kids?
4. [ ] Let's invite your parents for lunch next Sunday.
5. [ ] Hello. I'm at the supermarket, but I can't carry all the shopping on the bus.
6. [ ] Oh, no! We've just missed the last bus.
7. [ ] Hi, Dad. I'm afraid I've lost my mobile phone.
8. [ ] Oh, no. I haven't got enough money to buy this tablet today.

a OK, shall I phone for a taxi, then?
b Good idea. I'll call them this evening to see if they're free.
c Good idea. I'll go to the travel agent's tomorrow.
d Don't worry. I'll buy you a new one for your birthday.
e Oh, that's a pity. Shall I lend you some money?
f Don't worry. I'll bring the car and meet you there in ten minutes.
g Shall we go to the new Harry Potter film?
h OK, so we won't go to an Indian restaurant, then.

b Underline the correct words to complete the sentences.

1. **A** Will / <u>Shall</u> / Won't we go to the cinema tonight?
   B Yes, OK. I 'll / won't / shall check which films are on and phone you back.
2. **A** Hi, Dad. I've missed the last bus home!
   B Don't worry. I shall / won't / 'll bring the car into town and meet you by the cinema.
3. What will / shall / won't we do this weekend?
4. Don't worry. The station's very near here, so you 'll / shall / won't miss your train.
5. **A** Shall / Will / Won't we try and get tickets for The Rolling Stones concert?
   B Good idea. I won't / shall / 'll phone the ticket office.
6. Look, I know you're a vegetarian, so I 'll / won't / shall cook steak for dinner.
7. Will / Won't / Shall I help you do the washing-up?
8. **A** Let's take Monica and Sara to that new Chinese restaurant this evening.
   B Yes, that's a great idea. I 'll / won't / shall call them and reserve a table for 7:30.

2 VOCABULARY Adjectives: places

a Complete the crossword puzzle.

→ **Across**

4. Stonehenge is an ___ancient___ monument in Wiltshire in England. It's about 5,000 years old.
5. When the weather is really bad, we play on the i_____ tennis court at my local sports centre.
7. There are lots of h_____ mountains in Switzerland. For example, the Matterhorn is about 4,500 metres above sea level.
8. I live in a very o_____ town. Tourists never come here!
10. We live in a p_____ village. There's no traffic at all!

↓ **Down**

1. My school's in a really m_____ building. It's only five years old.
2. This road is very n_____. It isn't wide enough for a bus.
3. The view from the top of the Empire State Building is m_____.
6. It's very n_____ in this café, isn't it? It's difficult to hear you.
9. The British Museum is h_____. There are nearly 600 rooms!

b Choose the opposites of the adjectives in **bold**. Use the words in the box.

| modern | high | pretty | outdoor | quiet | ~~wide~~ |

1. The streets in the old part of town are very **narrow**. ___wide___
2. I think the new houses they've built are really **ugly**. _____
3. There is a big **indoor** swimming pool in my town. _____
4. That restaurant's always very **crowded**. _____
5. This is one of the most **ancient** cities in Greece. _____
6. The hills in the South of England are quite **low**. _____

3 PRONUNCIATION
Sound and spelling: want and won't

a ▶4.3 Listen and underline the correct words to complete the sentences.

1. We won't / <u>want to</u> go swimming today.
2. They want to / won't take you to the old castle.
3. I won't / want to go to that restaurant again.
4. You want to / won't wait for the next train.
5. I won't / want to study English again next year.
6. Tom and I want to / won't invite him to our party.

23

4C Everyday English
Are you doing anything on Wednesday?

1 USEFUL LANGUAGE
Making arrangements

a Put the conversation in the correct order.

- [ ] **A** Oh, OK, never mind. How about Friday? Is that OK for you?
- [ ] **B** Brilliant! 11 o'clock. See you then.
- [ ] **A** OK, so you can't do this week. What are you doing next Monday?
- [ ] **B** Oh, that sounds nice. I'll just check. No, sorry, I can't do Wednesday. I'm going shopping with my mother.
- [1] **A** Are you doing anything on Wednesday? Would you like to go for a coffee?
- [ ] **B** Next Monday? Just a moment, I'll just check. Nothing! I can do next Monday. Perfect!
- [ ] **A** Great! So we can meet for a coffee on Monday?
- [ ] **B** Friday … hang on a minute … no, sorry. I'm going to London for the day. This week's really busy for me.
- [ ] **A** Shall we meet at The Coffee Place at 11.00?
- [ ] **B** Yes, Monday's fine. Where shall we go?

b ▶4.4 Listen and check.

c Put the words in the correct order to make sentences.
1 like / would / bring / me / anything / you / to ?
   Would you like me to bring anything?
2 anything / doing / you / Saturday / this / are ?
   _____
3 busy / us / week's / really / this / for .
   _____
4 come / we / what / round / shall / time ?
   _____
5 you / on / doing / next week / Tuesday / are / what ?
   _____
6 round / you / come / would / for / to / lunch / like ?
   _____
7 can't / Thursday / I / this week / do .
   _____
8 for / Sunday / is / OK / you / this ?
   _____

d ▶4.5 Listen and check.

Debbie's diary

Monday	am	9–11 meeting at work
	lunch	1–2 lunch with Mum
	pm	
Tuesday	am	7–9 fitness class
	lunch	
	pm	6–8 cinema with Joe
Wednesday	am	8–9 yoga
	lunch	
	pm	6.30 doctor's appointment
Thursday	am	
	lunch	12–1 shopping with Karen
	pm	7–8.30 dance class
Friday	am	
	lunch	all day – work conference
	pm	
Saturday	am	
	lunch	day off!
	pm	
Sunday	am	day trip to Blackpool
	lunch	
	pm	

e Read Debbie's diary and underline the correct words to complete the telephone conversation.

SANDRA Hi, Debbie! Are you free to meet on Monday morning?
DEBBIE I'll just check my diary. I'm sorry, I have a [1]*fitness class / meeting / doctor's appointment* then.
SANDRA Oh, that's a shame. How about Monday lunchtime?
DEBBIE No, I'm having lunch with [2]*Joe / Mum / Karen* then.
SANDRA Never mind. Are you doing anything on Tuesday evening?
DEBBIE I'm afraid I'm going [3]*shopping / to the cinema / to a dance class*.
SANDRA That sounds like fun! Let's see. I'm busy on Wednesday and Thursday. Could we meet on Friday?
DEBBIE Unfortunately, I'm busy all day on Friday. I've got a [4]*doctor's appointment / dance class / work conference*.
SANDRA OK. What are you doing on Sunday?
DEBBIE Oh, dear. On Sunday I'm [5]*at a work conference / in Blackpool / in a meeting* all day.
SANDRA So you don't have any free time this week?
DEBBIE Yes, I do! I have the whole day off on [6]*Wednesday / Thursday / Saturday*!

2 PRONUNCIATION Sentence stress

a ▶4.6 Listen to the sentences and underline the stressed words or syllables.
1 I can't meet you tomorrow.
2 He can meet us at the station.
3 I didn't understand him.
4 She hasn't seen that film.
5 I must start cooking dinner.
6 They don't like basketball.

24

4D Skills for Writing
Are you free on Saturday?

1 READING

a Read Abby's email to Tony and his reply, and tick (✓) the correct answer.
- a ☐ Abby invites Tony and Laura to come to a birthday party at her house.
- b ☐ Abby and Mike would like to go to a Chinese restaurant with Tony and Laura.
- c ☐ Abby wants to see Tony and Laura's new house.
- d ☐ Abby invites Tony and Laura to celebrate Mike's birthday at a Chinese restaurant.

Hi Tony

How are things? We haven't seen you for ages. I hope you and Laura are well and that you're enjoying your new house.

Are you doing anything on Friday, 21st June? It's Mike's 40th birthday and we're going to our favourite Chinese restaurant, Xian, with some friends. We're going to book a table for eight o'clock. Can you come? It would be lovely to see you both and have a chance to chat.

Everyone's bringing an old photo of Mike. Could you bring your favourite photo of Mike from when he was at school or university?

Love

Abby

Hi Abby

Lovely to hear from you. Yes, we're well and we love our new house. We've just finished painting our bedroom and we're going to start on the kitchen next weekend.

Thanks for inviting us to Mike's birthday party. We're free on the 21st and we'd love to come. I'll bring some really funny photos of Mike when he was at school! We're looking forward to seeing you and Mike and having a chat.

All the best

Tony

---

b Read the emails again. Are the sentences true or false?
1. Abby and Mike have seen Tony and Laura recently.
2. Tony and Laura have recently moved to a new house.
3. Abby wants Mike's friends to take photos of him at the restaurant.
4. Tony and Laura are making some changes to their new house.
5. Tony doesn't have any old photos of Mike.

2 WRITING SKILLS Inviting and replying

a Correct the sentences. Use contractions where possible.
1. Hope you're well and your enjoying your new job.
   <u>Hope you're well and you're enjoying your new job.</u>
2. Thanks for invite me to your party.
3. It would be lovely to seeing you.
4. We're free on Saturday and we love to come.
5. This is just to say that we have a party on Saturday.
6. We didn't see you for ages!

3 WRITING

a Read Sam's email to Jess inviting her to his birthday party, and the notes below. Decide whether Jess can or can't go to the party and write her reply.

Hi Jess

How are you? I haven't seen you for over six months. I hope you are well and enjoying your new job.

Are you doing anything next Saturday? I'm having a birthday party at my house and I'm inviting a few friends. People are arriving at 7:30. Everyone is bringing some food for the party. Could you bring a salad?

It would be lovely to see you and have the chance to chat.

Love Sam

Notes for reply:
She CAN go to the party
1. Me? Fine. Give information about new job
2. Thanks for invitation
3. Free next Sat, love to come
4. Bring a huge salad!
5. Looking forward, nice chat

Notes for reply:
She CAN'T go to the party
1. Me? Fine. Give information about new job
2. Thanks for invitation
3. Party = fun! Can't come
4. Visit cousin in Paris next weekend
5. Enjoy the party!

25

UNIT 4
Reading and listening extension

1 READING

a Read the magazine article. Put the events in the correct order that Julia does them.

- ☐ Arriving at the theatre
- ☐ Getting a new outfit
- ☐ Going to the hairdresser's
- ☐ Having lunch
- ☐ Meeting my friend
- ☐ 1 Running on Venice Beach

b Read the magazine article again. Are the sentences true or false?

1. There are lots of people on Venice Beach in the morning.
2. Julia thinks she will spend all day shopping.
3. There are lots of people at the shopping mall.
4. Julia doesn't want to have lunch until she's bought a new dress.
5. Julia is looking forward to the evening because she has never been to a premiere before.

c Complete the sentences with the correct forms of the verbs in brackets.

1. Julia __is meeting__ her friend at the shopping mall today. (meet)
2. At 1:15 Julia is _____ lunch. She _____ anything yet. (have, buy)
3. At 4:22 Julia _____ the hairdresser's in a taxi. (go)
4. At 6:35 Julia _____ to go out. (get ready)
5. At 7:15 she _____ at the theatre. (arrive)

d Write an email to a friend about your plans for the weekend. Remember to include:

- where you are going
- what you are going to do
- who you are going with
- what you think will happen.

12 HOURS IN LOS ANGELES
with film director Julia Fitzgerald

7:15 am The sun is shining, and I'm going to put my tracksuit on and go for a run. I love this time of the day as it's so peaceful and quiet down on Venice Beach.

10:00 am I'm going to a film premiere tonight so I have to look my best. I've arranged to meet my friend at an indoor shopping mall in Santa Monica, but she's not here yet. It's a modern place with lots of great shops and some pretty little cafés. I'd like to buy a new dress. It's crowded today, so I'm sure we'll be here all day!

1:15 pm We've stopped for lunch at an ordinary LA diner. I haven't bought anything yet, but all this walking around is making me hungry. I'm going to get a burger and fries.

2:20 pm My friend's taking me to a huge new department store, which sells everything. She thinks we'll find something in here.

3:05 pm Success! I've found a gorgeous red dress and matching high heels. We've decided to celebrate with coffee and cake at my favourite outdoor café near the beach.

4:22 pm I'm in a taxi now. I've got an appointment at the hairdresser's at 4:30 pm. I hope I won't be late. I think I might be!

6:35 pm I'm nearly ready. Shall I wear the gold bracelet and necklace or the black one? I can't decide. The car is coming at 7:00 pm so I have a bit of time.

7:15 pm We're driving up to the theatre for the premiere. It's crowded and noisy as everyone is hoping to see all the stars. It's my first time at a premiere so I'm so excited. It's going to be a brilliant night!

2 LISTENING

a ▶4.7 Listen to the conversation. Complete the sentences with the names in the box.

| Alex Giles's mum Gavino ~~Giles~~ Isaac |

1 ___Giles___ is going to finish university this summer.
2 _____ is marrying an Italian woman.
3 _____ is teaching Giles Italian next week.
4 _____ wants to go sightseeing in Rome.
5 _____ is going on a date tonight.

b ▶4.7 Listen to the conversation again and tick (✓) the correct answers.

1 Why is Giles going to Italy this summer?
   a ✓ He is going to a wedding.
   b ☐ His girlfriend is Italian.
   c ☐ He wants to visit Rome.
2 Who is Laura?
   a ☐ Giles's girlfriend.
   b ☐ Alex's fiancée.
   c ☐ A student in their class.
3 What is Giles's dad going to do if Giles passes his exams?
   a ☐ He's going to pay for Italian lessons.
   b ☐ He's going to buy him a new suit.
   c ☐ He's going to take him to Rome.
4 What does Isaac like about Rome?
   a ☐ The new buildings.
   b ☐ The history.
   c ☐ The mix of old and new architecture.
5 Where is Isaac going now?
   a ☐ He is going to meet a girl.
   b ☐ He is going to get a haircut.
   c ☐ He is going home.

c Write about what you're going to do when you finish your English course. Include the answers to these questions:
   • Where are you going to go?
   • What would you like to do?

Review and extension

1 GRAMMAR

Correct the sentences.

1 I going to look for a job in a hotel this summer.
   I'm going to look for a job in a hotel this summer.
2 Don't worry. I pay the money back tomorrow.
3 He'll go to buy a new car next month.
4 Will I come to your house in half an hour?
5 Will we go to that café for a cup of tea?
6 Are you going to doing your homework this evening?

2 VOCABULARY

Correct the sentences.

1 They've got a fantastic outside swimming pool in my town.
   They've got a fantastic outdoor swimming pool in my town.
2 Are you going to buy a new suit case in the sales?
3 I love it here in the country. It's so peacefull!
4 He always uses a tie when he goes for a job interview.
5 I love coming to this park because you can't hear the traffic. It's so quite here.
6 That restaurant's so noise. It's really hard to talk there.

3 WORDPOWER look

Complete the sentences with the words in the box.

| after forward up around ~~at~~ for |

1 He looked __at__ the timetable to see when the next train left for London.
2 Excuse me. I'm looking _____ a bank. Is there one near here?
3 We're really looking _____ to seeing our Spanish friends tomorrow.
4 We have a lovely babysitter that looks _____ our children when we go out for the evening.
5 I'm tired! Do you really want to look _____ the museum again?
6 If you aren't sure what it means, look _____ the word in your dictionary.

REVIEW YOUR PROGRESS

Look again at Review your progress on p.46 of the Student's Book. How well can you do these things now?
3 = very well   2 = well   1 = not so well

I CAN ...

talk about my plans for celebrations	☐
plan a day out in a city	☐
make social arrangements	☐
write and reply to an invitation.	☐

27

5A I have to work long hours

1 VOCABULARY Work

a Complete the sentences.
1 This person looks after the plants and cuts the grass. g ardener
2 When your hair gets too long, you make an appointment with this person. h_____
3 If you have a problem with your central heating, you need to call this person. p_____
4 This person works in a laboratory and might have a university degree in chemistry or biology. s_____
5 Somebody whose job is to look after people's money. b_____
6 If you have a problem with the lights in your house, you call this person. e_____
7 If the police arrest you, this person can help you. l_____
8 This person can help you to manage your money. a_____
9 This person checks your teeth to make sure they are in good condition. d_____
10 When you are in hospital, this person looks after you. n_____

b Complete the sentences with the words in the box.

team   people   environment   self-employed   skills
salary   university degree   qualifications   training
~~long hours~~

1 He's usually in his office from 8 am until 8 pm, but he doesn't mind working _long hours_.
2 She works for an important bank in London, earns a very good _____ and drives a company car.
3 You need to have several years of _____ to become a doctor.
4 They have a really nice working _____ – their offices are modern with good air conditioning and plenty of light.
5 I really enjoy working on big projects with lots of other people. It's good to work in a _____.
6 You need to have a _____ to become a lawyer.
7 Receptionists have to deal with _____, so they need to be friendly and polite.
8 Some people prefer to be _____ and work for lots of different companies.
9 Secretaries need to have a lot of _____ – they need to be organised, and good with computers.
10 You need to have good _____ if you want to get a job at this university.

2 GRAMMAR must / have to / can

a Complete the sentences about the signs with *have to* or *can't*.

> ALL VISITORS MUST WASH THEIR HANDS BEFORE ENTERING THIS ROOM.

> PASSENGERS MUST NOT STAND UP UNTIL THE PLANE HAS COMPLETELY STOPPED.

1 You __have to__ wash your hands before you go into this room.
2 Excuse me, madam. You _____ stand up until the plane has stopped.

> VISITORS MUST NOT TAKE PHOTOS USING FLASH PHOTOGRAPHY.

> PASSENGERS MUST WEAR THEIR SEAT BELTS AT ALL TIMES.

3 I'm sorry, sir. You _____ take photos in here with a flash.
4 Excuse me. I'm afraid you _____ wear your seat belt all the time.

> YOU MUST WEAR A HARD HAT AT ALL TIMES ON THIS CONSTRUCTION SITE.

> YOU MUST NOT SMOKE IN THIS TOILET.

5 Visitors _____ wear hard hats when they come to this building site.
6 I'm sorry. You _____ smoke in the toilet.

b <u>Underline</u> the correct words to complete the text.

I work as a receptionist in a big hotel, so I [1]*must* / mustn't / can* always be polite to the guests. During the week, I [2]*don't have to / can't / must* go to bed late because I have to start work early. Fortunately, I [3]*don't have to / mustn't / can't* wear a uniform, but I [4]*can / mustn't / have to* dress smartly.

My sister's a student, so she [5]*mustn't / doesn't have to / can't* get up early most days. However, she [6]*doesn't have to / mustn't / has to* study very hard at the moment because she's got important exams next month.

My dad's a taxi driver, so he often [7]*has to / mustn't / can't* work in the evenings and at weekends. He [8]*doesn't have to / mustn't / must* drive fast because there are speed cameras everywhere in my town.

My mum's a nurse, so she [9]*has to / mustn't / can't* wear a uniform when she's at work. Sometimes she starts work very early but my dad usually takes her to work in his taxi, so she [10]*must / doesn't have to / mustn't* get the bus.

5B I might get a job today!

1 GRAMMAR
will and *might* for predictions

a Match 1–8 with a–h to make sentences.

1. [c] She might
2. [ ] I think I'll
3. [ ] Spain might not
4. [ ] I don't think she'll
5. [ ] I'm sure he'll
6. [ ] France won't
7. [ ] He might not
8. [ ] I might not

a win the match on Saturday. The Brazilian team are just as good as them.
b pass his exams. He's very clever and he's worked really hard all year.
c feel better tomorrow. She says she's taken some medicine.
d get to school on time. I've only just woken up!
e pass his exams. He hasn't worked very hard this year.
f win the match on Saturday. They haven't got any good players in their team and Brazil are a fantastic team.
g come this evening. She's not feeling well.
h see them tonight. We all usually go to the gym on Thursdays.

b Complete the sentences with *will* (or *'ll*), *won't*, *might* or *might not*.

1 I'm sure you __will__ pass your exams. You've worked very hard this year.
2 Don't go on holiday next week. They _____ invite you for a second interview.
3 I know they _____ offer me a good salary. A friend of mine works there and he doesn't earn a lot of money.
4 You _____ get a job immediately when you finish university – 50% of university graduates don't have a job three years after finishing their studies.
5 She doesn't think she _____ go travelling after university. She wants to find a job as soon as possible.
6 **A** Do you think he _____ pass all his exams?
   B Yes, I'm sure he _____. Don't worry.
7 Who knows? You _____ make some useful contacts at the conference.
8 I'm sure he _____ get the job. He doesn't have any experience.

2 VOCABULARY Jobs

a Write the names of the jobs under the pictures.

1 __builder__ 2 _____ 3 _____ 4 _____
5 _____ 6 _____ 7 _____ 8 _____
9 _____ 10 _____ 11 _____ 12 _____

b Complete the sentences with the correct jobs.

1 When I was little, I wanted to be a __vet__ because I loved looking after animals.
2 I'm looking for a good b_____ to fix the roof on my house.
3 Nick is a fantastic m_____. He can play the piano, the guitar, the cello and the saxophone.
4 Christopher Wren was the a_____ who designed St Paul's Cathedral in London.
5 Louise works in a department store as a s_____ a_____.
6 Johnny Depp is an American film a_____, famous for his role as Jack Sparrow in the *Pirates of the Caribbean* films.
7 Val works as a c_____, looking after old people in their homes.
8 Sarah works in our IT Department as a c_____ p_____.
9 James was a well-known j_____ who worked for *The New York Times* newspaper.
10 Yves St Laurent was a famous French fashion d_____.
11 Our p_____ always delivers the mail to our house at ten o'clock.
12 I hope that the p_____s in the UN can solve the world's problems one day.

29

5C Everyday English
I'll finish things here, if you want

1 USEFUL LANGUAGE
Offers and suggestions

a Put the words in the correct order to make sentences.
1. money / I / you / some / lend / the bus / for / shall ?
   Shall I lend you some money for the bus?
2. off / maybe you / ask / manager / for / your / should / the day .
   _____
3. Internet / look up / I'll / the / the / train times / on .
   _____
4. do / a taxi / guest / you / our / me / to / want / for / book ?
   _____
5. drive / airport / don't / the / why / I / to / you ?
   _____
6. arranging / about / a / in / meeting / Milan / how ?
   _____
7. money / don't / why / borrow / from / some / you / your father ?
   _____
8. Rome / could / direct flight / you / a / to / catch .
   _____

b ▶5.1 Listen and check.

c Complete the sentences with the words in the box.

| fine about could mind ~~shall~~ sorry matter |
| don't maybe would idea worry |

1. **A** _Shall_ I book a room for your meeting?
   B Yes, good _____.
2. **A** _____ you like me to drive you to the station?
   B No, I'll be _____. Don't _____ about it. I can take the bus.
3. **A** But you won't be able to have any lunch.
   B Oh, never _____. I'm not really hungry.
4. **A** I'm really _____. I can't come to the cinema tonight.
   B Oh, it doesn't _____. We can go another time.
5. How _____ asking your boss if you can have more time for the report?
6. Why _____ I book the train tickets on the Internet?
7. _____ you should invite your boss to the meeting, too?
8. You _____ send her some flowers for her birthday.

d ▶5.2 Listen and check.

2 PRONUNCIATION
Sentence stress: vowel sounds

a ▶5.3 Listen to the sentences. Tick (✓) which vowel sounds you hear for the modal verbs in **bold**.

	Strong vowel /ʊ/	Weak vowel /ə/
1 **Would** you like a coffee?		✓
2 Yes, I **would**. Thanks.		
3 **Could** you help me with my report?		
4 Yes, of course I **could**.		
5 You **should** get a taxi.		
6 Yes, you're right. I **should**.		
	/æ/	/ə/
7 **Shall** I book a meeting room?		
8 Well, what do you think? **Shall** I?		

5D Skills for Writing
I am writing to apply for a job

BRISTOL EVENING POST – jobs section

1 READING

a Read the job advert and Martin's job application, and tick (✓) the correct answer.

a ☐ The job is for 12 months.
b ☐ The job is in a hotel in Bristol.
c ☐ The hotel needs a receptionist.
d ☐ The hotel needs a waiter.

HOTEL RECEPTIONIST WANTED

We're looking for a hard-working and friendly receptionist to work in a hotel in Devon this summer. You will need to speak a foreign language.

We prefer someone with experience of working in hotels.

Accommodation and meals provided.

Apply online at www.bayviewdevonhotel.com by 31 May.

Subject: Hotel Receptionist

Dear Sir/Madam,

I am writing to apply for the job of receptionist at the Bay View Hotel, which you advertised in the Bristol Evening Post.

I am studying French and Spanish at Bath University and am available to work in July and August.

I would like to work for you because it would be a good opportunity for me to learn new skills and to work in a team. I have worked in a hotel before, as a waiter, so I have experience of dealing with customers and working in a busy hotel environment.

I attach a copy of my CV with details of my previous experience.

Could you please send me information about the salary, the working hours and the accommodation?

I look forward to hearing from you.

Yours faithfully,

Martin Evans

b Read the job advert and job application again. Are the sentences true or false?

1 The hotel will give the receptionist a bedroom and food.
2 People who apply for this job don't need experience of working in hotels.
3 Martin is free to work this summer.
4 Martin would like to learn some new skills.
5 Martin doesn't have any previous experience of working in hotels.
6 Martin would like more details about the job.

2 WRITING SKILLS Organising an email

a Match 1–8 with a–h to make sentences.

1 [g] I'm writing to
2 ☐ I have five years'
3 ☐ I would like to work for your company
4 ☐ I have a lot of experience of
5 ☐ My experience of working in a busy hospital
6 ☐ I attach a copy of my CV with
7 ☐ Could you please send me information
8 ☐ I look forward to

a working in a team and dealing with customers.
b about the working hours and the training programme?
c more information about my past employment.
d because it would be a good opportunity to learn some new skills.
e hearing from you.
f experience of working as a secretary in a busy hospital.
g apply for the job of secretary.
h will be very useful for this job.

3 WRITING

a Read the job advert and write a letter applying for the job.

The Argus – jobs section

SALES ASSISTANT WANTED

T-World are looking for a hard-working sales assistant to sell all types of computers, tablets, game consoles, smart TVs and smartphones in our brand-new superstore in Brighton.

We are offering a good salary plus sales bonus to the right person.

You will need previous sales experience and a good understanding of the latest technology.

We prefer someone with experience of working in a busy environment.

Full training programme given.

Apply by 30 September to salesassistant@tworld.co.uk

UNIT 5
Reading and listening extension

1 READING

a Read the article. Match the people 1–4 with pictures a–d.
1. ☐ Malcolm
2. ☐ Freya
3. ☐ Cara
4. ☐ James

a   b   c   d

b Read the article again and tick (✓) the correct boxes. Sometimes there is more than one possible answer.

	gets paid well	works and studies	is doing something he/she loves	has to work many hours every day
1 Malcolm		✓		
2 Freya				
3 Cara				
4 James				

c Read the article again and underline the correct answer. Sometimes there is more than one possible answer.
1. Who works for themselves?
   a Malcolm b Freya c <u>Cara</u> d James
2. Who doesn't earn any money?
   a Malcolm b Freya c Cara d James
3. Who has free weekends?
   a Malcolm b Freya c Cara d James
4. Who likes the place where he/she works?
   a Malcolm b Freya c Cara d James
5. Who studies and works in a different place?
   a Malcolm b Freya c Cara d James

d Write a paragraph about a job you'd like to do. Remember to include:
- the things you'd like to do in the job
- the hours
- the salary
- the environment.

Which way now?

When you leave school or university you must think carefully about what you would like to do next. Here, some young people tell us their experiences.

I thought about my skills and qualifications, and then about me. I've always liked working in a team, I like being outside and I decided I can't work in an office every day. Someone suggested I train to be a builder. I go to college Monday and Friday, and work Tuesday to Thursday. I have to get up early so I can't go out in the evenings, but I'm learning a useful skill.

Malcolm, 19

I love art and design and I've always wanted to do something I enjoy. I decided to study to become an architect. I'm learning so much and I'm doing what I want, which is really important. I have to study every day of the week and I just hope I can find a job when I leave university.

Freya, 21

I work for a number of companies as a book designer. I'm self-employed, which means I work on my own and not in a team. When I'm very busy I have to work long hours, in the evenings and sometimes at weekends. But I really like my job, and I can work at home, so I can say that I have a really nice working environment! I don't have to deal with customers or a manager! When I'm busy I can earn a very good salary, but I'm not always busy.

Cara, 28

I've always liked animals. Earning a really good salary is important to me too, so I studied to be a vet. I have to work long hours and I must study at home most weekends, but I know it is worth it when I'm helping sick animals.

James, 24

Review and extension

1 GRAMMAR

Correct the sentences.

1 Tomorrow's Sunday, so I mustn't get up early.
   Tomorrow's Sunday, so I don't have to get up early.
2 Excuse me, sir. You don't have to smoke on the plane. It's against the law.
3 Do you must wear a suit to work?
4 When I finish school, I can go to university. It depends on my grades.
5 I've to start work at 7 o'clock in the morning in my new job!
6 I'll take my umbrella. It can rain this afternoon.

2 VOCABULARY

Correct the sentences.

1 In your new job, I'm sure they'll give you lots of trainings.
   In your new job, I'm sure they'll give you lots of training.
2 My sister works as a shop assistent in a big department store.
3 You need good qualification if you want to become a doctor.
4 He works as a disigner for a top fashion magazine.
5 If you want to become a plummer, you'll need to go to college.
6 My brother wants to become a professional music.

3 WORDPOWER job and work

Underline the correct words to complete the sentences.

1 My GPS doesn't <u>work</u> / job very well when I drive through the mountains.
2 I've found a really good job / work in the local newspaper.
3 No, I can't go to the cinema. I've got to stay late at job / work.
4 My headache's a bit better, so I think that aspirin's beginning to work / job.
5 What time do you start job / work in the mornings?
6 He's got to work / job all weekend on that report.
7 I'm studying for my final exams – it's really hard job / work.
8 My dad's got a lot of small jobs / works to do in the garden.
9 My dad can't work / job out how to use the camera on his new phone.

2 LISTENING

a ▶5.4 Listen to the conversation. What did Josh say about these jobs? Tick (✓) the correct boxes. Sometimes there is more than one possible answer.

	Postman	Hairdresser	IT worker	Bank clerk
1 Work long hours	✓			
2 Nice working environment				
3 Deal with people				
4 Earn a good salary				
5 Work in a team				

b ▶5.4 Listen to the conversation again and complete the table to show what Josh liked and disliked about the jobs. Write one word in each space.

	He liked …	He disliked …
1 Postman	working <u>outside</u>	starting work _____
2 Hairdresser	learning new _____	dealing with _____
3 IT worker	_____ work when he wanted.	working at _____

c Choose one of the following:

1 Write a conversation between two people. Person A is interviewing Person B for the job of a journalist. Person B explains why he/she is the right person for the job, and asks five questions about the job. Person A asks questions and answers the questions Person B asks.
2 Write about the parts of a job you would be happy to do and what you definitely wouldn't like to do.

REVIEW YOUR PROGRESS

Look again at Review your progress on p.56 of the Student's Book. How well can you do these things now?
3 = very well   2 = well   1 = not so well

I CAN …

talk about what people do at work ☐
talk about my future career ☐
make offers and suggestions ☐
write a job application. ☐

6A You should have a break

1 GRAMMAR Imperative; should

a Complete the text with the words in the box.

| should go | don't use | eat | should read | shouldn't drink |
| go | don't sit | should have | shouldn't have | ~~get~~ |

Here are some ideas for those of you who have problems sleeping:

First of all, ¹ _get_ plenty of exercise during the day. For example, ² _____ for a long walk at lunchtime or after work. ³ _____ at home watching TV all evening. Secondly, you ⁴ _____ your dinner late in the evening. ⁵ _____ dinner at least four hours before you go to bed. Also, you ⁶ _____ coffee in the evening – it will stop you from sleeping. Next, ⁷ _____ your laptop or your tablet when you're in bed. Instead, you ⁸ _____ a good book at bedtime – it's very relaxing. Also, some people find it hard to sleep if their room isn't dark enough, so you ⁹ _____ thick curtains in your bedroom so that the light doesn't wake you up too early in the morning. Finally, you ¹⁰ _____ to bed at the same time every night. Doing this tells your body that it's time for you to go to sleep. Sweet dreams, everyone!

b Rewrite the sentences. Use *should*, *shouldn't* or the imperative.

1 He shouldn't listening to music while he's studying.
   He shouldn't listen to music while he's studying.

2 To eat lots of fruit and vegetables every day.
   _____

3 Not use your computer for very long in the evenings.
   _____

4 You should to try to relax for an hour before you go to bed.
   _____

5 I think she should getting more exercise during the day.
   _____

6 You don't should go swimming immediately after lunch.
   _____

7 When you've got a headache, to take an aspirin.
   _____

8 Don't stay you at work after 6 o'clock.
   _____

2 VOCABULARY Verbs with dependent prepositions

a Match 1–8 with a–h to make sentences.

1 [e] When you called me, I was looking
2 [ ] The train from Manchester arrived
3 [ ] Can you think
4 [ ] He was listening
5 [ ] Could you deal
6 [ ] He asked his father
7 [ ] Matthew decided to talk
8 [ ] My father wants to pay

a for £50 because he needed a new shirt for the wedding.
b to his son's teacher about his exam results.
c for the meal with his credit card.
d of a nice present for your grandfather's birthday?
e at an old photo of when we were at school.
f with this order for six takeaway pizzas, please?
g to the football match on the radio.
h at Euston Station 25 minutes late.

b Underline the correct words to complete the sentences.

1 In my job I have to deal *about / for / <u>with</u>* customers all day long.
2 It's hard to concentrate *with / on / for* my homework when you're listening to the radio.
3 This bus is crowded! I'll wait *for / to / from* the next one.
4 His girlfriend's gone to Paris for a month, so he thinks *from / about / for* her all the time.
5 They don't pay you much, do they? You should ask your boss *from / on / for* more money.
6 Jackie says she spends about £200 a month *at / on / to* clothes!
7 If you want to buy a new car now, you should borrow some money *with / for / from* your bank.
8 He's really generous. He paid *with / for / of* my plane ticket to New York!

3 PRONUNCIATION Sound and spelling: /uː/ and /ʊ/

a ▶6.1 Listen to the sentences. Are the vowel sounds in **bold** long /uː/ or short /ʊ/? Tick (✓) the correct box for each sentence.

	long /uː/	short /ʊ/
1 We t**oo**k my grandmother to the theatre.	☐	✓
2 The children wanted to go to the z**oo**.	☐	☐
3 Where did you l**o**se your mobile phone?	☐	☐
4 W**ou**ld you like a cup of coffee?	☐	☐
5 Wh**o** did you invite to the party?	☐	☐
6 I don't think you sh**ou**ld go to work today.	☐	☐
7 C**ou**ld I borrow £5, please?	☐	☐
8 What did you think of the f**oo**d?	☐	☐

6B I was very frightened

1 VOCABULARY -ed / -ing adjectives

a Underline the correct words to complete the sentences.
1. I thought the Tokyo metro was really *confused* / *confusing*. All the signs were in Japanese!
2. The football match was very *exciting* / *excited*. It finished 4 – 4.
3. Tracy isn't very *interesting* / *interested* in computer games.
4. I was *shocked* / *shocking* when I saw him. He looked very ill.
5. She was very *annoyed* / *annoying* when he asked her for some more money.
6. The flight from London to Mexico City was very *tired* / *tiring*.
7. I thought the view from the top of the Eiffel Tower was *amazing* / *amazed*.
8. He felt *embarrassing* / *embarrassed* when his mother kissed him in front of his friends.

b Complete the sentences with adjectives ending in *-ed* or *-ing*.
1. The people in the flat above me are so a<u>nnoying</u>. They play loud music when I'm trying to get to sleep.
2. He looked really c_____ when he woke up. He said, 'Where am I?'
3. I thought that TV documentary about Martin Luther King was so i_____.
4. The exam results were very s_____. Nobody got more than 50%!
5. She was very f_____ when she saw the spider, but she calmed down when we told her it was made of plastic.
6. He was very d_____ that his father didn't bring him a present from Spain.
7. They couldn't speak a word when they heard the s_____ news that the king was dead.
8. She felt very e_____ when he told her that they were going on holiday to Florida.

2 GRAMMAR Uses of to + infinitive

a Put the words in the correct order to make sentences.
1. job / I / to / disappointed / get / not / was / the .
   <u>I was disappointed not to get the job.</u>
2. sharks / was / learn / interesting / it / to / about .
   _____
3. our cars / you / tell us / park / where / can / to ?
   _____
4. wear / is / not / dangerous / to / a seat belt / it .
   _____
5. her / relax / to / she / a bath / help / had .
   _____
6. the station / went / to / meet / aunt / to / they / their .
   _____
7. her father / she / him / to / some money / ask / for / phoned .
   _____
8. didn't / he / what / to the party / know / wear / to .
   _____

b Correct the sentences.

1. They wanted buy him a nice birthday present.
   <u>They wanted to buy him a nice birthday present.</u>
2. He asked me how getting to the airport.
   _____
3. She was annoyed to not receive an invitation to his wedding.
   _____
4. They went to the supermarket for buy some food for dinner.
   _____
5. We couldn't remember which bus catching for the airport.
   _____
6. John and Angela decided to have not their wedding in Scotland.
   _____
7. It was embarrassing fail my driving test again.
   _____
8. She went to the library for borrow a book on dinosaurs for her son.
   _____

6C Everyday English
What do you think I should do?

1 USEFUL LANGUAGE
Asking for and giving advice

a Match sentences 1–8 with responses a–h.
1. [d] I think it's a good idea to book a table. The restaurant might be full.
2. [ ] Someone stole my handbag when I was at the beach this afternoon.
3. [ ] I'd speak to your boss about it.
4. [ ] I wouldn't worry too much. You can get a new passport at the embassy.
5. [ ] Do you think I should invite Steve to the surprise party?
6. [ ] What do you think I should do?
7. [ ] I didn't get the job in marketing.
8. [ ] I broke my finger on Saturday.

a. Oh, what a pity. I'm sure you'll get another job soon.
b. Oh, that's a shame. So that means you can't play tennis today?
c. No, I don't think that's a very good idea. Anna doesn't like him very much.
d. Yes, I suppose so. Saturday night can be very busy.
e. How awful! I'm really sorry to hear that.
f. I don't think I should do that. She'll be angry with me.
g. Yes, you're right. I can go there one day next week.
h. I think you should go to the police station.

b ▶6.2 Listen and check.

c Put the words in the correct order to make sentences.
1. apply for / which / should / do / job / you / I / think ?
   <u>Which job do you think I should apply for?</u>
2. colleagues / should / I / your / you / think / ask .
   _____
3. sorry / really / that / hear / to / I'm .
   _____
4. new job / a / should / do / think / I / you / look / for ?
   _____
5. I / a / think it's / to / your boss / speak / to / good idea .
   _____
6. about / talk / I'd / your parents / it / to .
   _____
7. apply / I / for / marketing job / new / the / wouldn't .
   _____
8. think / I / you / your / don't / job / leave / should .
   _____

d ▶6.3 Listen and check.

2 PRONUNCIATION Main stress

a ▶6.4 Listen to the sentences and tick (✓) the stressed words.
1. You're from Canada, right?
   a [ ] You're   b [✓] Canada
2. Elena works in the Spanish Embassy.
   a [ ] Spanish   b [ ] Embassy
3. Would you like to work in London?
   a [ ] work   b [ ] London
4. We're having a surprise party for Anna.
   a [ ] party   b [ ] Anna
5. My boss wants to speak to me.
   a [ ] boss   b [ ] me

36

6D Skills for Writing
I often worry about tests and exams

1 READING

a Read Anthony's email to Sue and Sue's reply. Tick (✓) the correct answer.

- a ☐ Anthony is looking for a new job.
- b ☐ Anthony doesn't want Jim to leave his job.
- c ☐ Sue gives Anthony some ideas to help him.
- d ☐ Sue works as a manager in a bank in London.

Dear Sue

The problem is that I'm feeling very stressed about my job at the moment. You see, Jim, one of the people in my team, has just left. They haven't replaced Jim yet and so my boss has given all of his work to the other people in the team, including me. Do you have any advice for me?

Regards

Anthony

Dear Anthony

Thank you for your email. I'm very pleased that you have written to me for advice.

This kind of situation is very common in companies when somebody leaves. I remember this happened when I was working in a bank in London. One summer, two of the people in my team left the bank at the same time. We had to do all of their work and it took three months to replace them! Anyway, here are some ideas that might help you.

First of all, try not to get too stressed about the situation. I think you should discuss the problem with your colleagues. Maybe they will have some ideas about how to make the situation a bit easier? Secondly, when you've got too much work to do, I think it's a good idea to try to prioritise your work carefully. For example, are there some less urgent jobs that you could do later?

Next, I think you should speak to your boss about this problem. He might not realise how much work he has given you and maybe he can find some other people to help you with it. Finally, I'd try to do something relaxing after work, such as going to the gym or swimming. It's important to relax when you aren't at work and to get plenty of sleep.

I hope this helps you and please feel free to come and talk to me in my office.

Best wishes

Sue Smith

HR Manager

---

b Read the emails again. Are the sentences true or false?

1 Anthony is doing all of Jim's work.
2 Sue was the manager of a team of two people at the bank.
3 Sue thinks that Anthony should talk to his colleagues about the problem.
4 Sue doesn't think Anthony should discuss the problem with his manager.
5 Sue thinks it's a good idea for Anthony to relax after work.

2 WRITING SKILLS Linking: ordering ideas and giving examples

a Put *for example* or *such as* in the correct place in each sentence. Add capital letters and punctuation (. , ') and make any other necessary changes.

1 There are lots of ways to make new friends joining a sports club.
   <u>There are lots of ways to make new friends, such as joining a sports club.</u>

2 It's a good idea to read something in English every day. You can read the BBC news pages on the Internet.
   _____

3 Why don't you do something relaxing this evening going for a swim after work?
   _____

4 There are more enjoyable ways of preparing for an exam. You could revise with a friend on the same course.
   _____

5 You could start a new hobby to help you relax dancing or swimming.
   _____

3 WRITING

a Read Kento's message to his English teacher, Tina. Use the notes below to write Tina's reply.

Dear Tina

I think I'm quite good at reading and writing in English, but listening is very hard for me. I really want to improve my listening. Do you have any ideas?

Thank you

Kento

Notes for message to Kento:
Paragraph 1: say thanks
Paragraph 2: me: learning Japanese – listening v. difficult – explain why – ideas to help …
Paragraph 3:
1) impossible to understand every word – concentrate on most important words
2) extra practice – study centre – CDs, e.g. CDs from Student's Book
3) radio / TV in English, films (+ subtitles)
4) podcasts – short stories?
5) pop songs + read words – find internet sites
Paragraph 4: hope this helps – talk to me after class?

37

UNIT 6
Reading and listening extension

1 READING

a Read the magazine article and underline the correct people to match the adjectives.

1 annoyed — Petra / <u>manager</u> / Sue
2 embarrassed — Petra / customers / Sue
3 confused — manager / Sue / Petra
4 frightened — Petra / manager / customers
5 not disappointed — customers / Petra / Sue
6 surprised — Petra / customers / Sue

b Read the magazine article again. Tick (✓) the correct answers.

1 What is Petra's problem?
   a ☐ She doesn't like spending time with customers.
   b ✓ Her manager thinks she works too slowly.
   c ☐ She gets confused by what the customers say to her.

2 Who is Toni?
   a ☐ One of Petra's customers.
   b ☐ Petra's manager.
   c ☐ Another hairdresser.

3 When does Petra get embarrassed?
   a ☐ When her manager gets angry with her in front of customers.
   b ☐ When the customers talk to her.
   c ☐ When her manager looks at her.

4 What surprises Sue?
   a ☐ That Toni talks to Petra in front of customers.
   b ☐ That Toni doesn't understand the customers.
   c ☐ That Toni doesn't understand what good customer service is.

5 What does Sue suggest?
   a ☐ She suggests that Petra tells her manager how she feels.
   b ☐ She suggests that Petra doesn't think about it.
   c ☐ She suggests that Petra's customers speak to Toni.

c Read the magazine article again. Match 1–5 with a–e to make sentences.

1 [c] Petra thinks that a customer who
2 ☐ Toni thinks that Petra
3 ☐ Petra can't concentrate when Toni
4 ☐ Petra is confused because she
5 ☐ Sue thinks that Toni

a keeps looking at her.
b shouldn't spend so much time talking to customers.
c spends a lot of money should get good service.
d thinks she is very good at her job.
e will change his mind after the customers speak to him.

d Write an email to Petra giving her some advice about her problem. Remember to include:
- some advice
- some instructions
- a similar situation from your own life.

Ask Sue

Every week, our experts answer your problems. This week, Sue Taylor, our writer and management expert, answers a question about a problem at work.

Dear Sue
I need to ask you for some help.
I'm a hairdresser and I work in a very fashionable salon. I'm very good at dealing with the customers and I like to talk to them when I cut their hair. They pay a lot of money for their haircuts, and I think it's important to spend time with them and make sure they're happy. But my manager, a man called Toni, gets really annoyed with me and keeps telling me to work faster. He sometimes talks to me in front of the customers, which makes me really embarrassed. He looks at me all the time when I talk to them and now I find it really difficult to concentrate on what I'm doing.
I'm really confused. I'm a really good hairdresser, none of the customers are ever disappointed with my work and I get on well with all my colleagues. I'm frightened of losing my job if I say anything.
Can you help me?
Petra

Dear Petra
You're right. When customers spend a lot of money on a haircut, they should enjoy the experience, feel relaxed and get excellent service. I'm surprised Toni doesn't understand this. How many of your customers would come back if you spent less than 15 minutes with them?
I think you should ask your customers for help. Ask them to speak to or write an email to your manager telling him what they like about the service you give them. I think your manager will soon change his mind.
Good luck!
Sue

2 LISTENING

a ▶6.5 Listen to three friends talking about studying. Tick (✓) the people that match the statements.

	Georgia	Marsha	Max
1 I can't study at home.	✓		
2 I study in the library.			
3 I haven't got a good memory.			
4 I listen to a recording of myself to help me remember.			
5 I can help someone with their revision.			

b ▶6.5 Listen to the three friends talking about studying again. Tick (✓) the correct answers.

1 What is Georgia's problem?
   a ✓ Her brother is disturbing her.
   b ☐ She hasn't got a laptop to use for studying.
   c ☐ She doesn't want to go to the library to study.
2 What does Max suggest Georgia do?
   a ☐ She should go to the library to study.
   b ☐ She must tell someone to stop.
   c ☐ She should ask her parents to help her with the problem.
3 What is Georgia going to do?
   a ☐ Talk to someone about the problem.
   b ☐ Go somewhere else to avoid the problem.
   c ☐ Talk to someone and go somewhere else.
4 Who has a problem with History?
   a ☐ Georgia.
   b ☐ Max.
   c ☐ Marsha.
5 What is Georgia embarrassed about?
   a ☐ Her poor memory.
   b ☐ Making a song to help her revise.
   c ☐ Her marks in the Physics exam.
6 What is Marsha's problem?
   a ☐ She is confused by a subject.
   b ☐ She doesn't want to study a subject.
   c ☐ She has to take a subject again next year.

c Write to somebody giving advice about how he or she can get better exam results.

Review and extension

1 GRAMMAR

Correct the sentences.
1 You shouldn't to drink coffee before you go to bed.
   You shouldn't drink coffee before you go to bed.
2 I think he should doing some exercise every day.
3 You should read a book for to help you relax.
4 She asked me drive her to the station.
5 My father taught me how play the guitar.
6 What I should do if I can't sleep very well?

2 VOCABULARY

Correct the sentences.
1 The football match was really excited. It finished 3 – 3.
   The football match was really exciting. It finished 3 – 3.
2 I was thinking in that TV programme I saw last night.
3 My uncle paid the tickets and he bought popcorn for us as well.
4 I can't afford to spend a lot of money in a holiday this year.
5 My little sister isn't very interesting in fashion.
6 I didn't hear the phone because I was listening some music.
7 I didn't think that horror film was frightened. What about you?
8 I didn't have any money, so I had to borrow £20 to my brother.

3 WORDPOWER verb + to

Complete the sentences with the words in the box.

read   sold   paid   wrote   lent
described   ~~explained~~   brought

1 She __explained__ the problem to her parents.
2 I _____ £200 to Jack so he could buy a phone.
3 He _____ lots of CDs with him to the party.
4 Gianni _____ an email to the school to ask for information about their language classes.
5 We _____ £500 to the builder who fixed our roof.
6 She _____ the story very quietly to her class, closed the book and put it back in the cupboard.
7 They _____ their car to their neighbour for £1,500.
8 Laura _____ her new house in Australia to me.

REVIEW YOUR PROGRESS

Look again at Review your progress on p.66 of the Student's Book. How well can you do these things now?
3 = very well   2 = well   1 = not so well

I CAN ...

give advice on common problems	☐
describe extreme experiences	☐
ask for and give advice	☐
write an email giving advice.	☐

39

7A I'm the happiest I've ever been

1 GRAMMAR
Comparatives and superlatives

a Read the information in the table about London, New York and Rome. Complete sentences 1–8 with the correct forms of the adjectives in brackets.

	London	New York	Rome
Average max. daily temperature: January	8°C	3°C	12°C
Average max. daily temperature: July	23°C	29°C	30°C
Population	8.5 million	8.3 million	2.7 million
Size	1,500 km²	800 km²	1,300 km²
Average hotel price	$200	$220	$180

1 In July London isn't as ___warm___ as New York. (warm)
2 Rome is the _____ city in July. (hot)
3 New York is _____ than London in January. (cold)
4 Rome is less _____ than New York in February. (cold)
5 Rome has the _____ population. (small)
6 Rome isn't as _____ as London. (big)
7 London is _____ than New York. (large)
8 Hotels in New York are _____ than hotels in Rome. (expensive)

b Put the words in the correct order to make sentences.

1 job / as / isn't / new / my old one / interesting / my / as .
   My new job isn't as interesting as my old one.
2 film / it's / the / seen / exciting / ever / I've / most / I think .
   _____
3 happier / is / ever / she's / than / my sister / been .
   _____
4 to understand her / more / she speaks / quickly / because / you / it's hard / than .
   _____
5 one of / best / he / the USA / universities / to / in / went / the .
   _____
6 was / much warmer / the weather's / yesterday / it / than .
   _____
7 her sister / than / she / got / and / worked / in her exam / 95% / harder .
   _____
8 a year ago / English / speaks / than / much better / now / he .
   _____

2 VOCABULARY get collocations

a Underline the correct words to complete the sentences.

1 I *get together / get to know /* <u>*get on well with*</u> both of my sisters – we're very close.
2 I'm going to Australia on business next week, so I'll *get married / get in touch with / get to know* my friend Chris who lives in Sydney.
3 In 2003, he married a Japanese girl and decided to stay in Japan because he *got a place at / got a job / got an offer* as a language teacher in Tokyo.
4 When she went to live in Manchester, she *got to know / got better / got engaged* her neighbours very quickly because everyone was so friendly.
5 Annie and Tom *got married / got divorced / got together* after they met at a friend's birthday two years ago. It was love at first sight.
6 If you don't drink bottled water, you might *get ill / get better / get old* because the water isn't very clean in this area.
7 In my company, we normally *get rich / get paid / get an offer* on the last day of each month.
8 My parents *got married / got divorced / got engaged* last year, but they are still good friends.

b Complete the sentences with the correct forms of the expressions in the box.

get engaged	get rich	~~get better~~	get paid
get to know	get a place	get an offer	get married

1 Josh broke his leg playing football last year. Luckily, he ___got better___ very quickly and he's going skiing next month!
2 My parents _____ in 1985 and I was born in 1987.
3 He bought her a lovely silver ring when they _____ last month.
4 You might _____ at Oxford University if you study very hard and do really well in your exams.
5 He _____ when he sold his software company to Google five years ago.
6 Emma was working as a model in Paris when she _____ to be in a French film.
7 We _____ lots of really interesting people when we lived in San Francisco.
8 Brad Pitt _____ over $35 million for his last film.

40

7B I didn't use to eat healthy food

1 VOCABULARY Health collocations

a Match 1–8 with a–h to make sentences.

1. [c] She gave up
2. [ ] I've lost a lot of
3. [ ] I'm sure he's put on
4. [ ] My plan is to get
5. [ ] A lot of teenagers today are
6. [ ] She keeps in
7. [ ] It's important to have a healthy
8. [ ] I was a regular

a shape by exercising regularly and eating carefully.
b fit by going to the gym twice a week from January.
c smoking three years ago and now feels much healthier.
d overweight because they don't get enough exercise.
e smoker for 10 years but now I've stopped.
f weight since I started eating a healthy diet.
g weight because he doesn't look as slim as he did last year.
h diet with plenty of vegetables and fruit.

b Complete the sentences with the words in the box.

| lose | get | gave up | keeps | gone | put on |
| allergies | smoker | overweight | healthy |

1 She _keeps_ in shape by going to the gym twice a week and running.
2 He _____ a lot of weight a year ago. Now he's on a _____ diet and he looks fitter.
3 Have you ever _____ on a diet to _____ weight?
4 If you go swimming three times a week, you'll _____ fit very quickly.
5 My uncle sleeps better because he _____ drinking coffee last month.
6 His doctor told him he was _____ and that he should lose 10 kilos.
7 Do you have any _____ to certain types of food, such as seafood or peanuts?
8 She was a regular _____ for a long time, but she suddenly decided to stop last year.

2 GRAMMAR used to

a Rewrite the highlighted phrases. Use the correct forms of *used to*.

Twenty years ago, when I was a student, I use to live
[1] _I used to live_ in a large house with five of my friends. We usedn't to have [2] _____ much money, so we didn't used to go [3] _____ out to restaurants or clubs in the evenings.

Instead, we use to invite [4] _____ our friends to come to our house in the evenings. One of my friends, Sandro, was Italian and he use to cook [5] _____ fantastic meals for us, such as pizza or pasta. After dinner we used watch [6] _____ TV or listen to music together.

Another friend of mine, Jordi, used play [7] _____ the guitar and teach us beautiful Spanish folk songs. Fortunately, our neighbours not used to complain [8] _____ about the noise we made.

What about you? Used you to live [9] _____ with a group of friends when you were at university, or you used to live [10] _____ with your family?

b Complete the sentences with the correct forms of *used to* and the verbs in brackets.

1 We _used to have_ (have) a dog, but it died five years ago.
2 Molly _____ (buy) bread from the supermarket, but now she has to get it there because the baker's closed last month.
3 What _____ you _____ (eat) for lunch when you were at school?
4 She _____ (speak) German quite well, but she hasn't been there for 10 years and so she's forgotten most of it.
5 I _____ (go) to work by bus every day, but now I usually cycle or walk.
6 _____ you _____ (play) with dolls when you were little?
7 My grandfather _____ (have) a mobile phone until we bought him one for his birthday.
8 We _____ (watch) black-and-white films at the cinema when I was young. We thought they were brilliant!

41

7C Everyday English
It hurts all the time

1 USEFUL LANGUAGE
Doctors' questions

a Match the doctor's sentences 1–8 with the patient's responses a–h.

1. [d] So, what's the problem?
2. [ ] When did this start?
3. [ ] Where does it hurt? Can you show me?
4. [ ] Can I have a look? So, does it hurt here?
5. [ ] Are you taking anything for the pain?
6. [ ] Well, I don't think it's anything to worry about.
7. [ ] I think it's just indigestion.
8. [ ] I'll give you a prescription for some tablets. Take two every four hours.

a Just indigestion? What a relief!
b Fine, thanks very much. Goodbye.
c Phew! That's good to hear.
d I've got a stomach ache. It's very painful.
e Yes, it does. It hurts all the time. I can't get to sleep.
f Yes, I've taken some aspirin.
g About two days ago.
h Here, in this area.

b ▶7.1 Listen and check.

c Complete the sentences with the words in the box.

| relief | taking | ~~worry~~ | you'll | problem | hear |
| ~~nothing~~ | sick | hurts | look | shouldn't | get |

1. Don't _worry_. It's _nothing_ to worry about.
2. Phew! That's good to _____.
3. It _____ all the time. I can't _____ to sleep.
4. Can I have a _____?
5. Are you _____ anything for the pain?
6. I feel _____ and exhausted.
7. I think _____ need to see another doctor.
8. So, what's the _____?
9. What a _____!
10. You _____ stay in bed.

d ▶7.2 Listen and check.

e Put the conversation in the correct order.

[ ] Yes! Very much. Is it broken?
[ ] OK, Doctor. Thank you.
[ ] Can you show me where it hurts?
[1] So what brings you here today?
[ ] Does it hurt if I touch it here?
[ ] Right here, next to my wrist.
[ ] I've hurt my arm. I fell off my bike.
[ ] No, I don't think so. I'll put a bandage on it.

2 PRONUNCIATION
Tones for asking questions

a ▶7.3 Listen to the questions. Put a tick (✓) to show if the doctor's voice go up ↗ or down ↘ at the end.

	↗	↘
1 Do you do any exercise?	✓	
2 When did this problem start?		
3 Could you take a few tests tomorrow?		
4 How many aspirins have you taken?		
5 How long have you had this problem?		
6 Are you taking anything for the pain?		
7 Do you have any allergies?		
8 Have you had any accidents recently?		

42

7D Skills for Writing
After that, I decided to make a change

1 READING

a Read Nicola's blog on the right and tick (✓) the correct answer.

a ☐ Nicola could speak Spanish very well two years ago.
b ☐ Nicola lives and works in Barcelona.
c ☐ Nicola wanted to get a new job as a manager.
d ☐ Nicola studied Spanish at university.

b Read the blog again. Are the sentences true or false?

1 Two years ago, Nicola didn't get on well with her colleagues at the bank.
2 Managers in Nicola's bank need to have a very good level of Spanish.
3 Nicola used to buy a Spanish newspaper every day.
4 Nicola studied Spanish at a language school in Barcelona.
5 Nicola is going to work for her bank in their Barcelona office.

2 WRITING SKILLS
Linking: ordering events

a Complete the blog below with the words in the box.

| then | the end | after | soon | a while | ~~first~~ |

How I became a top chef

Three years ago, I was a terrible cook. I could cook an English breakfast for my family, but I couldn't cook anything more exciting than that. Two years later, I got a job in a top London restaurant as a chef. Shall I tell you how I did it?

At ¹ _first_ , my wife helped me. She showed me how to make some simple dishes, such as roast chicken and potatoes and spaghetti bolognese. ² _____ that, I started going to cookery classes at a college in London, where I learned how to cook lots of different dishes from all over the world. ³ _____ I started inviting my friends to my house for dinner and I cooked some of the meals I learned at the college. After ⁴ _____, my friends told me I was a brilliant cook and that I should become a chef. ⁵ _____ I entered an important cookery competition on television and, to my surprise, I won! In ⁶ _____, I got an offer to work at The Ritz Hotel as one of their chefs, so I gave up my office job and I've never regretted it for one moment.

HOME | ABOUT | **BLOG**

NICOLA123

About two years ago, my job was getting really boring. I liked the bank and enjoyed working with my colleagues, but I needed a change. I wanted to become a manager because I thought the work would be more interesting and that I would have the chance to travel to different countries.

However, I knew that it was very important for managers in my bank to write and speak excellent Spanish. I studied Spanish at school, but I stopped when I was 16, so I couldn't remember much. I decided to try and improve my Spanish quickly so that I could apply for a job as a manager.

To begin with, I studied my old Spanish textbook from school and did lots of exercises. After that, I started reading Spanish newspapers online for 30 minutes every day and looked up the meaning of any new words in my dictionary. Soon I could understand nearly everything I read. After a while, I found a website where I could practise listening and speaking. Then I joined a Spanish class at a language school in my town and went to classes twice a week. In the end, after about 18 months, I could understand and speak Spanish quite well.

I decided to start applying for management jobs at the bank and last month I got an offer of a job in Barcelona. My new job starts in September, so I've got a few weeks to find a flat. I'm really excited about going to live in Spain.

3 WRITING

a Read the notes and write Kirsty's blog about how she changed her journey to work.

Notes for Kirsty's blog

2 years ago: go to work by bus = lots of traffic, 1 hour +
buy a bicycle? but not very fit

bought old bicycle from friend ...
1) frightened of cycling on road – so many cars & lorries
2) went to a park – cycled slowly, 5–10 mins.
3) house to local shops – 2 km
4) house to city centre – 5 km
5) everywhere on my bike

now: 8 km to work – feel fit & healthy
only 30 mins to work – save 1 hour a day

43

UNIT 7
Reading and listening extension

1 READING

a Read the magazine article. Match the numbered paragraphs 1–4 with the titles a–d.

1 Paragraph 1 — a How we used to eat
2 Paragraph 2 — b Not all about the money
3 Paragraph 3 — c Playing outside
4 Paragraph 4 — d Unknown dangers

b Read the magazine article again and underline the correct answers.

Maria thinks …
1 the streets *are* / *used to be* much quieter *now* / *in the past*.
2 the children *are* / *used to be* happier *now* / *in the past*.
3 people *have* / *used to have* healthier diets *now* / *in the past*.
4 more people *smoke* / *used to smoke* now / *in the past*.
5 people *are* / *used to be* richer *now* / *in the past*.

c Read the magazine article again and tick (✓) the correct answers.

1 Maria's family …
   a ☐ were very poor.
   b ☐ had better lives than their neighbours.
   c ✓ were normal for where they lived.
2 There was a party in the street …
   a ☐ before Maria got married.
   b ☐ when Maria got married.
   c ☐ when Maria met her husband.
3 People didn't use to go on a diet or need to get fit because …
   a ☐ they didn't like doing exercise.
   b ☐ they preferred to eat junk food.
   c ☐ they worked so much.
4 People used to smoke a lot because …
   a ☐ it was much cheaper.
   b ☐ they didn't understand it was dangerous.
   c ☐ you could smoke and buy cigarettes everywhere.
5 Maria thinks …
   a ☐ richer people are happier.
   b ☐ she would prefer to grow up now.
   c ☐ the Internet has made people's lives easier.

d Write about how your life has changed over the past ten years. Write about what you used to do and what you do now. Write about:
- your education
- your free time
- your friends and family.

Remembering the past

As she celebrates her 100th birthday, Maria Morales Cabrillo talks to *Youth2day* magazine about growing up.

1
My family didn't have much money, but my brothers and I had what we needed. We didn't feel poor. We were like everyone else around here. We used to get together with the other children and play in the street every day. We all got on well. It was a nice place to be. Everything used to happen in that street. I got to know my husband in the street. He lived opposite us. When we got engaged we had a party in the street. It was wonderful. It's changed a lot. It's a lot quieter now. The children don't play outside. I know their lives are busier, but I don't think the kids are happier. And they're fatter than we were! I can't believe that so many children are overweight these days.

2
We used to eat three times a day and no more. We had a much healthier diet. Lots of vegetables, some meat and very little sugar. There didn't use to be junk food like crisps and burgers and no one needed to go on a diet or get fit. Everyone on our street, children and adults, used to work so hard.

3
It wasn't all better. Lots of people smoked. We didn't know how bad smoking was. My husband was a regular smoker. Fortunately, he gave up smoking when our children were born.

4
My husband used to work in the local shoe factory. He worked hard but didn't get paid very much. It was difficult sometimes. People are richer and their lives are easier now, especially with the Internet. But our lives were happier then. I wouldn't change my life then for anything.

2 LISTENING

a ▶7.4 Listen to the conversation. Complete the table with the names in the box.

Dale George   Lisa Baker   Martin Dowd
~~Mike Andrews~~   Stephen Downes

	Name	20 years ago	Now
1	Mike Andrews	poor	rich
2		popular	popular
3		good looking	overweight and unhealthy
4		didn't like someone	is married to the person he didn't like
5		overweight	slim and healthy

b ▶7.4 Listen to the conversation again and complete the sentences. Write one word in each space.

1 Stephen Downes used to be __married__ to Jenny Robertson.
2 Jenny wanted Stephen to stop _____ and _____ coffee.
3 Lisa Baker has _____ a lot of weight and is a lot _____ than she used to be.
4 Lisa is going to get _____ to a German man.
5 Mike Andrews is a lot _____ than he used to be.
6 Dale George didn't use to _____ Nicola Walker.

c Write about your friends and family ten years ago. Remember to include:
- what they used to do
- what they used to look like
- what they used to be like.

Review and extension

1 GRAMMAR

Correct the sentences.

1 Ronaldo is one of the most famous footballers of the world.
   Ronaldo is one of the most famous footballers in the world.
2 I think São Paulo is the most biggest city in Brazil.
3 My brother didn't used to like coffee when he was a teenager.
4 This exercise is more easier than the last one.
5 I'm studying harder this year as last year.
6 London is the expensivest city in the UK.

2 VOCABULARY

Correct the sentences.

1 I think you should give out smoking if you want to get fit.
   I think you should give up smoking if you want to get fit.
2 You'll have to get a diet if you want to lose weight.
3 My brother has got a new job and he gets paying very well.
4 She loves her boyfriend and I think they'll get engage soon.
5 While he was at university, he got to knowing Sarah.

3 WORDPOWER *change*

Match 1–8 with a–h to make sentences.

1 [g] The waiter hasn't given you
2 [ ] OK, let's go and play tennis. You can change
3 [ ] If she doesn't like the dress, she can take it back
4 [ ] When you go away on holiday, it's better to change
5 [ ] We always go to Italy. Let's go to Greece
6 [ ] You should keep
7 [ ] To fly from London to Sydney, you usually have to
8 [ ] She planned to take the train to Edinburgh, but at the last minute she changed

a some change in your purse for the bus.
b this summer for a change.
c your money at a bank, not at the airport.
d her mind and took the plane instead.
e change planes in Bangkok or Kuala Lumpur.
f and change it for another one.
g the right change. You gave him £20, not £10.
h into your shorts and trainers in the toilets.

REVIEW YOUR PROGRESS

Look again at Review your progress on p.76 of the Student's Book. How well can you do these things now?
3 = very well   2 = well   1 = not so well

I CAN ...

talk about life-changing events	☐
describe health and lifestyle changes	☐
talk to the doctor	☐
write a blog about an achievement.	☐

8A My favourite book is based on a true story

1 VOCABULARY Art and music; Common verbs in the passive

a Look at the types of art, music and literature and label the pictures.

1. _poem_
2. _____
3. _____
4. _____
5. _____
6. _____
7. _____
8. _____
9. _____
10. _____

b Match 1–8 with a–h to make sentences.

1. [c] In the film *The Bourne Identity*, Jason Bourne was
2. [ ] The 19th-century novels *War and Peace* and *Anna Karenina* were
3. [ ] The first *Star Wars* film was
4. [ ] The opera *Carmen* by the composer Bizet was first
5. [ ] The play *Romeo and Juliet* by William Shakespeare was
6. [ ] The movie *Apollo 13*, starring Tom Hanks, was
7. [ ] The iPod was
8. [ ] You can see *Guernica* in a special gallery in the Museo Reina Sofía in Madrid. It was

a set in the town of Verona in Italy.
b performed in Paris in 1875.
c played by Matt Damon.
d directed by George Lucas in 1977.
e painted by Pablo Picasso in 1937.
f written by the Russian writer Leo Tolstoy.
g based on the true story of NASA's third mission to the moon.
h designed by Apple in 2001.

2 GRAMMAR The passive: present and past simple

a Complete the sentences about the Statue of Liberty. Use the present or past simple passive forms of the verbs in brackets.

The Statue of Liberty ¹ _is known_ (know) around the world as a symbol of America, but it ² _____ (not make) in America. It ³ _____ (design) in France by Frédéric Auguste Bartholdi. It ⁴ _____ (give) to the United States by the people of France. The statue's head and arm ⁵ _____ (finish) first. In fact, these parts ⁶ _____ (make) before the rest of the statue ⁷ _____ (design). At first, there wasn't enough money to finish the rest of the statue. Finally, enough money ⁸ _____ (find). Over 120,000 people helped to pay for the statue – most of them gave less than $1. The rest of the statue ⁹ _____ (create) in small pieces in France and the pieces ¹⁰ _____ (take) to America by ship. Finally, the statue ¹¹ _____ (put) together in New York. It ¹² _____ (finish) in 1886. These days, it ¹³ _____ (visit) by over 3.2 million tourists every year.

b Rewrite the sentences. Use the passive. Say who does/did the action only if this information is important.

1. They make Porsche cars in Germany.
   Porsche cars are made in Germany.
2. They built the Eiffel Tower in 1889.
   _____
3. George Orwell wrote the novel *Nineteen Eighty-Four* in 1949.
   _____
4. They held the 2012 Olympic Games in London.
   _____
5. Steven Spielberg directed the film *Schindler's List* in 1993.
   _____
6. They grow the best coffee in Colombia.
   _____
7. They sold two million new cars in the UK last year.
   _____
8. This factory produces 5,000 bicycles every year.
   _____

8B I've hated rugby since I was at school

1 GRAMMAR
Present perfect with *for* and *since*

a Complete the exchanges. Use the present perfect forms of the verbs in brackets and *for* or *since*.

1 A <u>Have you</u> (you) always <u>loved</u> (you, love) horses?
   B Yes, I _____ (love) horses _____ I was a little girl.
2 A _____ (you, live) in Cambridge _____ a long time?
   B Yes, we _____ (live) here all our lives.
3 A How long _____ (you, be) married to Sarah?
   B We _____ (be) married _____ 2005, but I _____ (know) her _____ longer.
4 A How long _____ (you, have) your stomach ache?
   B I _____ (have) it _____ last night.
5 A How long _____ (you, work) as a journalist?
   B I _____ (be) a journalist _____ over 20 years.

b Underline the correct words to complete the sentences.

1 We *'ve lived* / <u>lived</u> here for 10 years – from 1964 to 1974.
2 I *know* / *'ve known* Sam since we were at school together.
3 My daughter *'s been* / *was* in the USA for six weeks, but she's flying home from San Francisco tomorrow.
4 She *had* / *'s had* a headache since she woke up this morning.
5 I *'ve been* / *was* in Madrid since 2012, but before that I *worked* / *'ve worked* in Hong Kong for two years.
6 John *had* / *'s had* a motorbike since he was 16 years old.

2 VOCABULARY Sports and activities

a Which verb do we use to talk about each sport and activity? Complete the table with the words in the box.

<u>gymnastics</u> squash golf surfing yoga volleyball
athletics snowboarding ice skating tennis rugby
football aerobics jogging ice hockey rock climbing
karate skateboarding scuba diving windsurfing judo

play	go	do
		gymnastics

b ▶8.1 Listen and check.

c Complete the crossword puzzle.

→ Across
5 Why don't we play <u>volleyball</u> when we go to the beach? I've got a ball and the nets are already there.
8 The beaches in Wales are often very windy, so they're good for _____.
10 In New York, you can go ice _____ in Central Park in the winter.
11 My uncle sometimes goes rock _____ in the mountains.
12 When I'm stressed, I do _____. It helps me to relax.

↓ Down
1 I think that the most popular sport in Canada is ice _____.
2 I'm not very good at skiing, but I love _____ – it's great fun!
3 In my opinion, the best part of the Olympic Games is the _____. I love watching the 100 metres and the long jump.
4 My grandparents play _____ twice a week. They play all 18 holes, so it's a good way for them to keep fit.
6 Bondi Beach in Sydney is a great place to go _____.
7 I can't run very fast, but I like _____. Sometimes I run about four or five kilometres.
9 Have you ever been scuba _____ in the sea? I love seeing all the beautiful fish under the water.

3 PRONUNCIATION Word stress

a ▶8.2 Listen to the words and tick (✓) the stressed syllable in each word.

1 snowboarding
   a ✓ snow   b ☐ board   c ☐ ing
2 athletics
   a ☐ ath   b ☐ let   c ☐ ics
3 jogging
   a ☐ jog   b ☐ ging
4 gymnastics
   a ☐ gym   b ☐ nas   c ☐ tics
5 ice hockey
   a ☐ ice   b ☐ hoc   c ☐ key

8C Everyday English
I'm really sorry I haven't called

1 USEFUL LANGUAGE
Apologies and excuses

a Put the words in the correct order to make sentences.

1. to / for dinner / didn't / but / last week, / I / invite you / feel / I meant / well .
   I meant to invite you for dinner last week, but I didn't feel well.

2. your / I couldn't / party yesterday / was / come to / ill / because / I'm sorry, / I .
   _____
   _____

3. I / you / email / my computer / because / working / couldn't / wasn't .
   _____
   _____

4. didn't / be late / for / to / is / my watch / but / broken / mean / I / the meeting, .
   _____
   _____

5. but / haven't / really sorry / were / I / bought you / I'm / the shops / closed / a present, .
   _____
   _____

6. working / I / call you / but / my mobile / didn't / last night, / wasn't / I'm sorry .
   _____
   _____

7. going to / been / by today, / was / the report / but / finish / I've / I / so busy .
   _____
   _____

8. you / meant to / send / your address / I / find / a birthday card, / I couldn't / but .
   _____
   _____

b Complete the sentences with the words in the box.

| fault | had to | mean | ~~sorry~~ | couldn't | worry |
| fine | going to | matter | meant | | |

1. I'm really ___sorry___ I didn't phone you this morning.
2. I _____ send her any flowers for her birthday.
3. I didn't _____ to be so late.
4. It doesn't _____. It's _____.
5. I was _____ take you to a nice restaurant last night.
6. I _____ to come and visit you when you were in hospital.
7. Don't _____ about it. It wasn't your _____.
8. We were going to come yesterday, but we _____ visit our grandfather in hospital.

2 PRONUNCIATION
Tones for continuing or finishing

a ▶8.3 Listen to the sentences. Put a tick (✓) to show if the tone goes up ↗ or down ↘ at the end.

	↗	↘
1 I meant to send you an email	✓	☐
2 I'm sorry I didn't come to your party	☐	☐
3 I couldn't phone you last night	☐	☐
4 I had to stay late at work yesterday	☐	☐
5 Sorry, I didn't mean to make you worry	☐	☐
6 I was going to call you	☐	☐
7 I'm sorry I didn't reply to your message	☐	☐
8 I had to visit my grandmother yesterday	☐	☐

b ▶8.4 Does the speaker have anything more to say? Listen and check.

8D Skills for Writing
I couldn't put the book down

1 READING

a Read the review of *Nineteen Eighty-Four* and tick (✓) the correct answer.

The reviewer thinks that …
a ☐ the book isn't very interesting.
b ☐ the book is based on a true story.
c ☐ life in Oceania is described very well.
d ☐ the ending isn't very good.

Nineteen Eighty-Four was written by George Orwell in 1949 and is set in the future, in 1984. After a nuclear war, Great Britain has become part of the totalitarian state of Oceania and everybody is controlled by the Party and its leader, Big Brother.

Although Winston Smith works for The Ministry of Truth, he secretly hates the Party and would like to oppose Big Brother. One day he meets and falls in love with Julia, a woman who also works at The Ministry of Truth and secretly hates Big Brother. However, it is very dangerous for Winston and Julia to have a relationship because love is illegal in Oceania.

Nineteen Eighty-Four is a really exciting novel. It's interesting to read and it describes the world of Oceania and Big Brother very well, so you can really imagine what life is like in a future totalitarian state after a nuclear war. Winston and Julia are wonderful characters and their illegal love affair is described very well. You can really understand how they feel.

I couldn't put the book down and I thought the ending was very clever. I can definitely recommend it. It's the best novel I've read for ages!

b Read the review of *Nineteen Eighty-Four* again. Are the sentences true or false?
1 Big Brother is the leader of Oceania.
2 Everybody knows that Winston hates the Party.
3 The reviewer thinks that the story is a bit boring.
4 The reviewer thinks the descriptions of people's lives in 1984 are very good.
5 The reviewer thinks *Nineteen Eighty-Four* is a book other people should read.

2 WRITING SKILLS
Positive and negative comments;
Linking: *although*, *however*

a Complete the sentences with *although* or *however*.
1 _Although_ I enjoyed the novel, the story is quite complicated.
2 The descriptions of London during the war were so realistic. _____, sometimes they were a bit long and dull.
3 The story was quite exciting, _____ the book was too long for me to finish on holiday.
4 The characters were described very well. _____, there are so many of them that sometimes I forgot who they were.
5 _____ the ending was rather sad, I really enjoyed the book and would definitely recommend it.
6 It's a brilliant book, _____ the story is sometimes a bit hard to follow.

3 WRITING

a Choose one of the following:
1 Write a review of a book you've read. Describe the characters, the descriptions and the story, and give your opinion of the book.
2 Read the notes below and write a review of the children's novel, *War Horse*, by Michael Morpurgo.

Notes for book review
Book: *War Horse*
Author: Michael Morpurgo
Story summary:
– about horse called Joey, sold to British Army at beginning of First World War
– sent to France, ridden by Captain Nicholls
– Captain Nicholls killed in fighting, so Joey given to a younger soldier, Warren
– J becomes friends with another horse, Topthorn: lots of adventures
– later, J and T taken by Germans
– T killed, but J works for German army until end of war
Review:
– *War Horse* written for children, but really enjoyed it
– story: v. interesting
– characters: described v. well
– can imagine what WW1 was like
– beautiful story, but v. sad: made me cry
– happy ending: at end of war J returned to Albert (his original owner before J was sold to army)
– couldn't put it down – definitely recommend …

49

UNIT 8
Reading and listening extension

1 READING

a Read the article from a tourist brochure. Are the sentences true or false?
1. The Brighton Festival is for people who like reading, listening to music, seeing films and plays.
2. It is very easy to see an event in the festival.
3. Sam Lee writes most of the songs that he sings.
4. You can see Kaarina Kaikkonen's *Time Passing By* in an art gallery.
5. *Flathampton* is a town in a theatre.

b Read the article again and complete the table to show the correct events for the sentences. Sometimes there is more than one possible answer.

	To Sleep To Dream	Sam Lee	Kaarina Kaikkonen	Flathampton
1 This event is outside.			✓	
2 You can listen to music from the past.				
3 There is nothing to see at this event.				
4 The audience must help the actor.				
5 This event tells a story.				

c Read the article again. Tick (✓) the correct answers.
1. The Brighton Festival …
   a ☐ is a big party that happens on Brighton beach every May.
   b ✓ happens in many places in the city and people often have to join in.
   c ☐ happens in people's houses and is not for visitors to the city.
2. In *To Sleep To Dream*, …
   a ☐ the audience must listen very carefully.
   b ☐ the audience watch a film about music.
   c ☐ the actors can't see the audience.
3. The songs that Sam Lee sings …
   a ☐ were written while he was travelling around Britain.
   b ☐ were written by the musicians in his band.
   c ☐ were found while he was travelling around Britain.
4. *Time Passing By* …
   a ☐ is a painting of a clock in Brighton.
   b ☐ is made using things belonging to other people.
   c ☐ is a sculpture made of clocks.
5. *Flathampton* …
   a ☐ is a play where the audience helps build a town.
   b ☐ takes place in the town centre.
   c ☐ is a play about children living in a theatre.

d Write a paragraph about a festival that happens near where you live. Remember to include:
- what it is
- where it is
- what happens
- what you like and dislike about it.

The Brighton Festival

If you like music, going to art galleries, the cinema or the theatre, or learning about books, then you really should visit the Brighton Festival. It has been going since 1965 and is now one of the largest arts festivals in England.

Come to Brighton in May and it's impossible not to see something as events, such as plays, concerts, films, dance performances and exhibitions, take place across the city in cinemas, theatres, galleries, the street, on the beach and even in people's own houses.

There have been some amazing events. Here are some of the highlights from the last two years:

Sam Lee is a singer who has spent many years travelling around Britain to find and listen to very old British songs. Many of the songs were written hundreds of years ago and he performs them with an interesting band of musicians.

Kaarina Kaikkonen is a Finnish artist who often uses other people's clothes to make large sculptures. In *Time Passing By*, the 23-metre high Clock Tower in the city centre was covered in clothes. It was very popular with visitors and artists.

In *To Sleep To Dream*, which was written by Daniel Clark, everyone in the audience wears a blindfold (something which covers the eyes so you can't see) to help them concentrate on the story, which is told with special 3D sound effects and music. In this film for the ears, your ears become your eyes.

Flathampton is a play with a difference. The whole theatre is turned into a town and the audience are taken through the town by the actors. As the story is told, the audience have to help make the buildings in the town that the actors perform in. It's been hugely popular with children and adults alike.

2 LISTENING

a ▶8.5 Listen to the conversation and look at the map of western Australia. Complete the table to show where the activities are. Sometimes there is more than one possible answer.

	Stirling Ranges	Perth	near Fremantle	Bunbury	Margaret River
1 This is for people who enjoy watching foreign films.		✓			
2 This is not for beginners.					
3 This is for people who don't mind getting wet.					
4 Lots of people will do this on Sunday morning.					
5 A group of young people will perform on a beach.					
6 This is for people who like sport.					

b ▶8.5 Listen to the conversation again. <u>Underline</u> the correct words to complete the sentences.

1 If you want to know where to go rock climbing at the Stirling Ranges, you can *look on the website* / <u>visit the information centre</u> / *visit your local bookshop or library*.
2 *The sea* / *The day* / *The river* affects where Margaret River Surfers meet.
3 The photographs in the art gallery in Perth were taken by *photographers* / *film directors* / *actors*.
4 On the beach at Wilson Park you can *listen to* / *write* / *read* poems by young poets.
5 *Jenny* / *Matt* / *Virginia* is going to be doing something active with a large group this weekend.

c Write about your hobbies. Remember to include:
- what you like doing
- how long you've been doing this
- where you do this
- who you do it with.

Review and extension

1 GRAMMAR

Correct the sentences.

1 The Harry Potter stories weren't written of Charles Dickens.
   The Harry Potter stories weren't written by Charles Dickens.
2 I knew Tanya since I was a child.
3 We've lived in Berlin since more than 10 years.
4 St Paul's Cathedral is designed by Christopher Wren.
5 I have taught at that university from 2010 to 2013.
6 I have played golf from I was twelve years old.

2 VOCABULARY

Correct the sentences.

1 This morning we played volley at the beach.
   This morning we played volleyball at the beach.
2 Skateboard is a great way for children to get fit.
3 Have you got a fotograph of your girlfriend?
4 Let's go golfing this afternoon.
5 These days, ice skate is popular in London during the winter.
6 When I was at school, I had to do gymnastic every Wednesday.
7 The *Mona Lisa* is one of the most famous paints in the world.
8 Let's go surf at the beach this afternoon.

3 WORDPOWER *by*

Complete the sentences with the words in the box.

bus   next Monday   hand   mistake   heart
~~the library~~   far   the way

1 She's waiting for you by *the library*.
2 By _____, are you doing anything on Friday?
3 Sorry, I clicked on SEND by _____ before I finished writing the email.
4 I usually come to work by _____.
5 Actors have to learn their lines by _____.
6 These shoes were made by _____. That's why they're more expensive.
7 Usain Bolt is by _____ the best 100 metres runner of the past ten years.
8 Please send me your report by _____.

REVIEW YOUR PROGRESS

Look again at Review your progress on p.86 of the Student's Book. How well can you do these things now?
3 = very well   2 = well   1 = not so well

I CAN ...

talk about music, art and literature	☐
talk about sports and leisure activities	☐
apologise, make and accept excuses	☐
write a book review.	☐

9A If I don't pass this exam, I won't be very happy

1 VOCABULARY Degree subjects; Education collocations

a Complete the crossword puzzle.

→ Across
3 He went to university to study D_rama_ and then got a job as an actor.
6 If you study L_____ at university, you will learn everything about our legal system.
7 If you want to become a manager in a large company, you should do a degree in M_____.
8 He was really interested in other people and how they think so he decided to study P_____.

↓ Down
1 She's doing a degree in E_____ because she wants to become a teacher.
2 He did a degree in A_____ and now he does beautiful drawings for children's books.
4 If you want to become a doctor, you'll probably have to study M_____ for five years at university.
5 She studied E_____ at university and now she's helping to design a new bridge across the River Thames.

b Complete the sentences with the words in the box.

| degree | get | notes | pass | revise | place |
| fail | essays | ~~marks~~ | handed | | |

1 He got really low _marks_ in his exams, so he's going to repeat the year.
2 She did a _____ in French and Spanish at university and now she works as a tourist guide.
3 I've got to write three _____ before the end of term and each one is 4,000 words long.
4 If she doesn't work hard this term, I think she might _____ her exams.
5 I've got to _____ for an important exam, so I won't go out today or tomorrow.
6 Because he _____ in his essay two days late, he only got a mark of 45%.
7 I didn't take a pen and paper with me to the meeting, but I took some _____ on my tablet.
8 He did extremely well in his exams and got a _____ at Harvard University.
9 Your daughter has always worked hard, so she'll definitely _____ into university.
10 You should study several hours each day if you want to _____ your exams.

2 GRAMMAR First conditional

a Put the words in the correct order to make sentences.

1 it / tomorrow, / we're / If / to / go skiing / going / snows .
   If it snows tomorrow, we're going to go skiing.
2 if / I'll / the USA / to / can / on holiday / I / a / cheap flight / find / go .
   _____
3 might / they / every day, / revise / they / their exams / If / pass .
   _____
4 at / If / her exams, / might / a place / she / in / Cambridge University / she / does well / get .
   _____
5 Medicine / have to / excellent grades / get / if / She'll / to / study / wants / at university / she .
   _____
6 call / tonight / tomorrow morning / him / if / doesn't / to / my email / I'll / reply / he .
   _____
7 on time / give / don't / you / bad mark / if / might / hand in / a / you / essay / Your teacher / your .
   _____
8 fail / university / your exams, / you / you / If / get into / won't .
   _____

3 PRONUNCIATION Word groups

a ▶9.1 Listen to the sentences and mark // where there is a pause.

1 I enjoy studying Maths at university, // but I hate taking exams.
2 If you take notes in the lesson, it will be easier to revise for the exam.
3 I'm going to work harder next year so that I get better grades.
4 If she fails her exam, she'll have to take it again in January.
5 Although he got excellent grades, he didn't get a place at Oxford University.

9B I managed to stop feeling shy

1 GRAMMAR Verb patterns

a Underline the correct words to complete the sentences.

1 I usually finish *to play / playing / play* tennis at about 9 o'clock.
2 We decided *not taking / not to take / to not take* the next train to Rome.
3 He keeps *to try / try / trying* to learn French, but he always gives up.
4 We wanted *see / to see / seeing* the film but there were no tickets left.
5 She promised *to not fail / not failing / not to fail* any exams this year.
6 I don't mind *not to have / to not have / not having* a holiday this year, if we can have one next year.
7 They learned *to speak / speaking / speak* English by talking to their grandfather.
8 I hope *go / to go / going* on holiday to France next summer.
9 I really enjoy *to spend / spend / spending* time with my family.
10 I worry about *to not do / not do / not doing* well in the exams, but I always pass.

b Complete the sentences with the correct forms of the verbs in the box.

meet   get   go   take   snow   ~~buy~~   read   play

1 He promised __to buy__ her a tablet if she got good grades in her exams.
2 We decided _____ the bus because the train was a lot more expensive.
3 I really enjoy _____ to the theatre when I'm in London.
4 She expected _____ a good result, but she didn't.
5 My children used to love _____ games on the beach when they were little.
6 She's arranged _____ him at the check-in desk at the airport.
7 He finished _____ his book and then went to bed.
8 It started _____ heavily last night and now they've closed the airport.

2 VOCABULARY Verbs followed by to + infinitive / verb + -ing

a Complete the sentences with the words in the box.

forgot   avoid   regretted   seemed   agreed
managed   ~~arranged~~   recommended   disliked
missed   refused   imagined

1 They __arranged__ to meet their friends outside the cinema at 7:30.
2 When we asked the tour guide, he _____ taking a taxi to the beach.
3 Because she was shy, she _____ meeting new people at parties.
4 She _____ to take her purse to the restaurant, so her boyfriend had to pay the bill.
5 Fortunately, the taxi driver _____ to drive us to the airport when we offered him 50 euros.
6 He _____ buying a house by the sea. He thought it would be lovely to walk on the beach every day.
7 After she moved from the UK to Australia, she really _____ seeing her family at Christmas.
8 I went to work early this morning because I wanted to _____ driving in the city centre during the rush hour.
9 Most of the hotels were full, but in the end we _____ to find a lovely hotel near the beach.
10 When she got low grades in her university exams, she _____ not working harder.
11 The hotel receptionist _____ to understand what I was saying because she brought some cheese sandwiches to our room five minutes later.
12 He _____ to leave the waiter a tip because the service was so slow.

b Underline the correct words to complete the sentences.

1 She has *avoided / agreed / missed* to meet Luke for a coffee after work.
2 He usually *avoids / missed / recommends* speaking to his neighbours because he's rather shy.
3 Let's *refuse / forget / arrange* to have dinner together one evening this week.
4 I'm sorry, but I *managed / forgot / refused* to get any bread when I was at the supermarket.
5 She *regrets / avoids / recommends* going to the Alhambra palace in Granada. She says it's beautiful.
6 Now that you live in a flat, do you *miss / regret / imagine* having a garden?
7 I don't want to go to the party, so if they ask me to go with them, I will *forget / manage / refuse* politely.
8 She *imagined / disliked / recommended* swimming in the sea because the water was always so cold.
9 Our baby *seems / manages / refuses* to prefer classical music to pop music.
10 Did you *refuse / manage / seem* to get some tickets for the concert? Most of them were sold on the first day.

53

9C Everyday English
Who's calling, please?

1 USEFUL LANGUAGE Telephoning people you know; Telephoning people you don't know

a Put the conversation in the correct order.

- **A** Is it possible to speak to Diane Smith, please?
- **B** Certainly, I'll just put you through.

- [ ] **C** Has she got your number?
- [ ] **C** OK. Shall I ask her to call you back?
- [ ] **C** No, I'm afraid she isn't available. She's in a meeting. Can I take a message?
- [ ] **A** Oh, hello. Is Diane there, please?
- [ ] **C** Yes, of course. Who's calling, please?
- [ ] **A** Yes, OK. Can you tell her that I called?
- [ ] **A** Yes, please. I'm here all morning.
- [1] **C** Hello, Diane Smith's phone.
- [ ] **A** This is Paul Roberts speaking.
- [ ] **A** Yes, she has.

- **C** Fine. I'll ask her to call you back.
- **A** Thanks. Bye.

b ▶9.2 Listen and check.

c Complete the conversation with the words in the box.

| got to go | I've got | is that | it's | just saying | soon |
| catch that | call you back | ring | good time | it is |

PAM Oh, hello, [1] _is that_ Tom?
TOM Yes, [2] _____.
PAM Hi, [3] _____ Pam here.
TOM Oh, hi, Pam.
PAM Is now a [4] _____ to talk?
TOM Well, I'm a bit busy.
PAM Sorry, Tom. I didn't [5] _____.
TOM Yes, I was [6] _____ that I'm busy. Sorry, but [7] _____ a meeting in five minutes. Can I [8] _____?
PAM Sure. Is everything OK?
TOM Yes, fine, but I've [9] _____.
PAM OK. [10] _____ me when you're free.
TOM Speak to you [11] _____. Bye.
PAM Bye.

d ▶9.3 Listen and check.

2 PRONUNCIATION
Main stress: contrastive

a ▶9.4 We can use contrastive stress to correct something someone else has said. Listen to the pairs of sentences. In each pair, tick (✓) the sentence where you hear a strong stress.

1. a [ ] The film starts at 8:50.
   b [✓] The film starts at 8:15.
2. a [ ] We're catching the 9 o'clock bus.
   b [ ] We're catching the 10 o'clock bus.
3. a [ ] My new boyfriend's name is James.
   b [ ] My new boyfriend's name is John.
4. a [ ] The programme is on BBC 1.
   b [ ] The programme is on BBC 2.
5. a [ ] We're going on holiday on Tuesday.
   b [ ] We're going on holiday on Thursday.
6. a [ ] I was born in 1990.
   b [ ] I was born in 1991.

54

9D Skills for Writing
Online courses are new to me

1 READING

a Read the profile of a French student on the right and tick (✓) the correct answer.

- a ☐ Claude's studying French.
- b ☐ Claude's going to study in the USA next year.
- c ☐ The online course is about American cinema.
- d ☐ Claude works in a café every day.

b Read Claude's profile again. Are the sentences true or false?

1. Claude likes the course he's doing at university.
2. He already speaks and writes English very well.
3. He hopes he will be better at writing in English after the course.
4. He wants to make friends with American students.
5. He doesn't often go to see films with his friends in Paris.

2 WRITING SKILLS
Avoiding repetition

a Change the words in **bold** in the sentences to pronouns.

1. I'm doing a degree in Medicine. I'm really enjoying **my degree** _it_.
2. The other students on my course all come from different countries. **The other students** _____ all speak English very well.
3. My cousin Sarah is also studying at the same university as me. **Sarah's** _____ doing a degree in Business Management.
4. When I'm not studying, I spend time with my girlfriend, Anna. I see **Anna** _____ three or four times a week.
5. We haven't decided which hotel to stay at when we go to Rome. I think we should try and find **a hotel** _____ near the Colosseum.
6. My dad's an IT consultant. **My dad** _____ usually works from home, but sometimes **my dad** _____ has to go for meetings in London.
7. My brother and I are both studying Law. My parents have always wanted **my brother and I** _____ to become lawyers, just like my father.
8. I've got a part-time job working in a supermarket. **This part-time job** _____ isn't very interesting, but I do **this part-time job** _____ because I need the extra money.

TELL US ABOUT YOU...

Hi everyone. My name's Claude and I'm French. I'm doing a degree in English and German at the Sorbonne University here in Paris. I'm really enjoying it. At the moment, I'm studying 20th-century American novelists, such as Ernest Hemingway. It's really interesting, but the best thing about my degree is that next year I'll spend six months in the UK and six months in Germany – I can't wait! I also get the chance to take an online course, in film studies. I can already speak English very well because my father's American. However, my written English isn't very good.

HOW DO YOU FEEL ABOUT THIS ONLINE COURSE?

I've always loved the cinema so I'm really looking forward to taking this American Film Studies course. I hope it will help me to understand American films better and also help me to improve my written English at the same time. I'm also very excited about making friends with students from different countries.

WHAT DO YOU DO WHEN YOU'RE NOT STUDYING?

I have a part-time job in a café near the Arc de Triomphe, in the centre of Paris. I work there three evenings a week and sometimes on Sundays, too. In my free time, I like going out with my friends. We usually go to the cinema, or sometimes we have dinner in one of the cheap restaurants in the Latin Quarter.

3 WRITING

a Read the notes and write a student profile for Hitomi, who is also taking the online American Film Studies course.

Student profile – notes

Tell us about you ...
- Hitomi: from Osaka, Japan
- Master's Degree in Economics – Tokyo University
- next year: job in London or New York?
- studied English at school: writing OK, but speaking???

How do you feel about this course?
- want to learn about Am. cinema: always loved Am. films
- improve English?
- talk about films with other students?
- my English: improve quickly?

What do you do when you're not studying?
sport – tennis x1 or x2 a week
 – golf at weekends
 – gym at the university: like keeping fit
 – yoga when stressed: helps me to relax

55

UNIT 9
Reading and listening extension

1 READING

a Read the text. Complete the sentences with the subjects in the box.

~~Business~~   Law   Medicine   Psychology

1. More foreign students study __Business__ than any other subject.
2. Li Jing is doing a degree in _____.
3. Mushtaq is studying _____.
4. Andreas is studying _____.

b Read the text again. Tick (✓) the correct answers.

1. The country with the most foreign students studying at its universities is …
   a ☐ China.
   b ☐ the UK.
   c ✓ the USA.
2. According to the British Council, the number of foreign students studying in the UK in ten years' time will be …
   a ☐ more than 126,000.
   b ☐ 430,000.
   c ☐ more than half a million.
3. Li Jing wanted to come to Britain …
   a ☐ a long time ago.
   b ☐ to study English.
   c ☐ to find a job.
4. Mushtaq decided to come to Britain because …
   a ☐ he came to school here.
   b ☐ he knows the country well.
   c ☐ he wanted to study Law.
5. How does Andreas feel about being in Britain?
   a ☐ He would like to be somewhere else.
   b ☐ He would like to stay here longer.
   c ☐ He prefers the food in Germany.

c Read the text again and complete the sentences. Write one word in each space.

1. If Mushtaq doesn't pass his __exams__, he will have to take the year again.
2. Li Jing imagined coming to _____ for a long time.
3. Andreas came to Britain because he _____ English.
4. Li Jing has recommended _____ in Britain to a friend of hers.
5. Andreas will try and find _____ here if he does well in his final exams.

d Write a paragraph about your experiences of studying. Remember to include:

- what you've studied
- where you've studied
- which exams you've taken
- what you like and dislike about studying.

STUDYING IN THE UK

| News | Sport | Weather |

Search

Over 430,000 foreign students from nearly 200 countries study at universities in the UK, with the largest number, over 78,000, coming from China. Only the USA takes more foreign students.

The most popular courses for foreign students are Business Studies and Engineering. Over 130,000 of those students do a degree in Business and more than 50,000 study Engineering in the UK.

A recent report by the British Council (a UK government organisation interested in British education and culture) suggests that over the next ten years an additional 126,000 international students will come to the UK to study. What makes the UK such an attractive place to study?

Li Jing, 19, Hong Kong
I decided to study in Britain because I love reading English novels and I've always dreamed about coming here. I applied to five universities in Britain and got a place at Edinburgh to study Medicine. I'm really happy with the course and I've met lots of students from all over the world. Edinburgh is a friendly city and I've already told my friend who would like to study abroad next year how good it is.

Mushtaq, 20, Pakistan
I studied at a British school in Pakistan and I've been to the UK many times. I have family in Manchester so it seemed to be a good choice for me. I'm doing a degree in Law. I have to write a lot of essays. At the end of the year I need to hand in three long essays and also pass my exams. I hope I manage to do everything. Failing the exams means repeating the year. I don't want to do that!

Andreas, 23, Germany
I wanted to study abroad and because English is the only foreign language I speak I decided to come here. I'm happy I came to England. It's close to Germany, and the culture and the food are similar. The countryside is beautiful and English people are quite friendly. I'm revising for my final exams in Psychology at the moment. If I pass, I'll probably stay here and look for a job.

Review and extension

1 GRAMMAR

Correct the sentences.

1 If I'll work hard, I'll pass the exam.
   If I work hard, I'll pass the exam.
2 I want that you buy me some bread and milk from the shop.
3 We won't play golf this afternoon if it will rain.
4 She enjoys to read books about dinosaurs.
5 Will you go to university next year if you'll get good grades?
6 I've just finished to have dinner with my family.

2 VOCABULARY

Correct the sentences.

1 When Robert left the UK to go and live in Australia, he regretted seeing his British friends.
   When Robert left the UK to go and live in Australia, he missed seeing his British friends.
2 He did well really at school and got into a good university.
3 She got a very bad note for her last History essay.
4 Although they worked hard, they both fell their Maths exam.
5 She always took taxis because she misliked waiting for buses.
6 He made a degree in Medicine and now he's a doctor.

3 WORDPOWER
Multi-word verbs with *put*

Complete the sentences with the prepositions in the box.

| on | down | up | off | ~~back~~ | through |

1 Please put the milk ___back___ in the fridge when you've finished with it.
2 They've put _____ the price of petrol again – it's so expensive!
3 David Jennings? Certainly, sir. I'll just put you _____.
4 OK, everybody. The exam has finished now, so please put your pens _____ and stop writing. Thank you.
5 It's raining quite hard now. Why don't we put _____ our game of tennis until tomorrow?
6 I usually put _____ a suit when I go for a job interview.

REVIEW YOUR PROGRESS

Look again at Review your progress on p.96 of the Student's Book. How well can you do these things now?
3 = very well   2 = well   1 = not so well

I CAN ...

talk about future possibilities	☐
describe actions and feelings	☐
make telephone calls	☐
write a personal profile.	☐

2 LISTENING

a ▶9.5 Listen to the conversation. Are the sentences true or false?

1 Gavino has written six essays this term.
2 Gavino is in his first year at university.
3 Gavino was late for class for two weeks.
4 Gavino failed his exams.
5 Gavino studies for the exam every Wednesday.
6 There are 25 students studying Psychology at the college in Gavino's year.

b ▶9.5 Listen to the conversation again. Match 1–6 with a–f to make sentences.

1 [b] The professor isn't going to mark Gavino's essay if
2 ☐ If Gavino doesn't come to class,
3 ☐ Gavino didn't go to some classes because
4 ☐ Gavino might not pass the exam if
5 ☐ Gavino might not be at the college next year if
6 ☐ The professor is not happy with Gavino because

a he doesn't come to every class.
b he doesn't hand it in on time.
c he fails the exam.
d he hasn't read any of the books.
e he was ill.
f he won't learn anything.

c Write about how you revise for an exam. Remember to include:
- how long you spend revising
- what you do to help remember information
- how good you are at doing exams.

57

10A Would you do the right thing?

1 GRAMMAR Second conditional

a Put the words in the correct order to make sentences.

1 I / to the police station / If / take it / found some money / in the street, / I'd .
   If I found some money in the street, I'd take it to the police station.

2 complain / the waiter / you / with your bill / Would / if / made a mistake ?
   _____

3 would / at school / there were / do / What / if / no teachers / you ?
   _____

4 I / I could / on petrol / cycled to work, / save / a lot of money / If .
   _____

5 did yoga / every day / I / feel / less stressed / I / would / if .
   _____

6 take a taxi / If / missed / the last bus, / I'd / have to / I .
   _____

7 if / I / could stop / became rich / working / I .
   _____

8 you / would / the film / download it / you / on the Internet, / found / If ?
   _____

b Underline the correct words to make second conditional sentences.

1 If I *would be* / *were* / *am* you, I *will buy* / *bought* / *would buy* her some flowers.
2 *Could you work* / *Will you work* / *Did you work* seven days a week if you *need* / *needed* / *would need* the money?
3 If the shop assistant *would be* / *was* / *will be* rude to me, *I'm complaining* / *I complained* / *I'd complain* to the manager.
4 *I could take* / *I'll take* / *I took* you to the station if my car *isn't* / *wasn't* / *wouldn't be* at the garage.
5 If you *will walk* / *would walk* / *walked* five kilometres every day, *you feel* / *you felt* / *you'd feel* much healthier.
6 If my new watch *stopped* / *will stop* / *would stop* working after two weeks, I *'ll take* / *'d take* / *take* it back to the shop.
7 I *didn't walk* / *wouldn't walk* / *won't walk* home by myself if I *am* / *would be* / *were* you.
8 What *did you do* / *do you do* / *would you do* if you *lost* / *would lose* / *will lose* your car keys?

2 VOCABULARY Multi-word verbs

a Match 1–8 with a–h to make sentences.

1 [h] Could you pass
2 [ ] Why don't you come
3 [ ] At some hotels you have to hand
4 [ ] My neighbour has agreed to take
5 [ ] As they were very tired, they didn't feel
6 [ ] I asked him to speak in English, but he carried
7 [ ] His mother looked
8 [ ] He was offered a great job, but he turned it

a down because he didn't want to leave Italy.
b after him when he was ill last week.
c care of my cats while I'm in hospital.
d in your passport when you first arrive.
e on speaking in German, so I couldn't understand him.
f like going to the cinema, so they watched a film on TV.
g round to my house for dinner on Saturday?
h on my complaint to the manager, please?

b Underline the correct words to complete the sentences.

1 It's very rude to carry *in* / *on* / *after* talking when the film begins.
2 When Jack lost his job, they decided to put *up* / *on* / *off* their wedding until he could find another one.
3 My neighbour came *round* / *after* / *to* for a cup of coffee this morning.
4 If you don't feel *down* / *like* / *off* eating much, just have a slice of toast with honey.
5 My sister's sad because she and her boyfriend broke *down* / *off* / *up* yesterday.
6 I found someone's mobile phone under my desk, so I handed it *in* / *on* / *up* to my teacher.
7 Who's going to look *up* / *for* / *after* your grandfather while your grandmother's away?
8 Can you pass *up* / *on* / *in* my message to Mr Henderson when he gets back on Monday, please?

3 PRONUNCIATION
Sentence stress: vowel sounds

a ▶10.1 Listen to the sentences and put a tick (✓) to show if the words in **bold** are stressed or unstressed.

	Stressed	Unstressed
1 If I had lots of money, I **would** buy an expensive sports car.	☐	✓
2 **Would** you marry him if he didn't live so far away?	☐	☐
3 If I were you, I **wouldn't** go swimming in the sea today.	☐	☐
4 If he asked her to go to Argentina with him, she probably **would**.	☐	☐
5 I **would** come and stay with you in New York if the flights weren't so expensive.	☐	☐
6 She **wouldn't** have to drive to work every day if she lived closer to her office.	☐	☐

58

10B I'm too embarrassed to complain

1 GRAMMAR
Quantifiers; too / not enough

a Underline the correct words to complete the conversation.

A We'll need ¹*much / a lot of / any* flour, sugar and, of course, carrots to make this cake. And also ²*a little / many / a few* orange juice.
B Well, there's ³*any / no / many* flour in the cupboard, so I'll have to go and buy some.
A Good idea. So, what else do we need? Er, butter … how ⁴*many / few / much* butter have we got in the fridge?
B Er, we haven't got ⁵*many / much / some* butter. Just one packet – 250 grams.
A OK, that's fine. And what about eggs – how ⁶*many / much / any* eggs are there?
B There aren't ⁷*much / many / any* eggs – only four.
A Oh, dear. And have we got ⁸*much / a little / any* carrots?
B Yes, I think we've got ⁹*a few / much / few* carrots, maybe three or four. Let me just check … oh, actually, there aren't ¹⁰*any / many / much* carrots. I think I ate the last one yesterday. Sorry!
A Never mind. OK, so can you also get me ¹¹*any / some / a little* carrots from the supermarket, please?
B OK, so you'd better give me a shopping list …

b Underline the correct words to complete the sentences.
1 I couldn't have a shower this morning because the water wasn't *enough warm / warm enough*.
2 There's *too much / too many* sugar in my coffee now – it's disgusting!
3 I'm sorry, I haven't got *enough milk / milk enough* to make coffee for everyone.
4 You're driving *too much / too* slowly – we won't get to the airport on time!
5 You aren't speaking *enough clearly / clearly enough*. I can't understand you.
6 There are *too many / too much* cars in London these days. The traffic's always terrible!
7 You're walking *too much quickly / too quickly* for me. I can't walk as fast as you.
8 My flat isn't *enough big / big enough* to have a birthday party for all my friends.

2 VOCABULARY Noun formation

a Complete the crossword puzzle.

→ **Across**
3 There isn't much c *hoice* in the little supermarket near me. For example, they only have two types of bread.
5 The directors took the d_____ to sell the company.
8 I buy books on the Internet. They're usually d_____ to my house within three or four days.
9 Excuse me. I'd like to make a formal c_____ about the quality of the food in this hotel.
10 I think people should always c_____ in a restaurant if the service is bad.

↓ **Down**
1 So you've ordered a new phone. What colour did you c_____ – black or white?
2 I've d_____ to redecorate my kitchen, so I've just been to the shop to buy some paint.
4 Our hotel was really horrible. It didn't match the d_____ they gave on the Internet.
6 Look how many people are in the q_____ for the new James Bond film. I don't think we'll be able to get tickets.
7 Why has the flight to Rio de Janeiro been delayed by five hours? Can you e_____ that to me?

3 PRONUNCIATION Word stress

a Tick (✓) the correct stress marking for each word.

1 decision
  a ✓ de**ci**sion
  b ☐ deci**sion**
2 enjoyment
  a ☐ en**joy**ment
  b ☐ enjoy**ment**
3 complaint
  a ☐ **com**plaint
  b ☐ com**plaint**
4 description
  a ☐ **des**cription
  b ☐ descrip**tion**
5 explanation
  a ☐ ex**pla**nation
  b ☐ expla**na**tion
6 delivery
  a ☐ de**li**very
  b ☐ deli**ve**ry
7 describe
  a ☐ **des**cribe
  b ☐ des**cribe**
8 complain
  a ☐ **com**plain
  b ☐ com**plain**

b ▶10.2 Listen and check.

59

10C Everyday English
Can I exchange it for something else?

1 USEFUL LANGUAGE Returning goods and making complaints

a Put the conversation in the correct order.

CUSTOMER	Good morning. Could you help me, please?
SALES ASSISTANT	Yes, of course. How can I help?
☐ CUSTOMER	Could I speak to the manager, please?
1 CUSTOMER	I'd like to return this DVD, please.
☐ SALES ASSISTANT	Do you have a receipt?
☐ SALES ASSISTANT	Would you like to exchange it for something else?
☐ SALES ASSISTANT	Well, I'm terribly sorry, but we don't give refunds without a receipt.
☐ CUSTOMER	No, I'm sorry, I don't. It was a present from my boyfriend, but I've already got it.
☐ SALES ASSISTANT	Yes, of course. I'll go and get him.
☐ CUSTOMER	No, I'd just like a refund, please.
MANAGER	What seems to be the problem?
CUSTOMER	I'd like to make a complaint.

b ▶10.3 Listen and check.

c Put the words in the correct order to make sentences.
1. but / excuse me, / ordered / isn't / what / this / I .
   Excuse me, but this isn't what I ordered.
2. ask / right away / I'll / that for / you / someone / to look at .
   _____
3. been here / still haven't / ordered / we've / but / for over an hour, / we .
   _____
4. they're / because / small / don't / these shoes / me / fit / a bit .
   _____
5. mind / I've / my / I've decided / keep it / changed / and / to .
   _____
6. to / I'd / for / exchange it / something else / like .
   _____
7. please / I'd / to / this watch, / return / like .
   _____
8. full refund / a / give / I'll / you .
   _____
9. hasn't been / helpful / sales assistant / your / very .
   _____

d ▶10.4 Listen and check.

2 PRONUNCIATION Sentence stress

a ▶10.5 Listen and decide where the main stress is in each question. Tick (✓) the stressed word.
1. Can you check my bill, please?
   a ☐ Can   b ✓ check
2. Would you like me to give you a refund?
   a ☐ like   b ☐ give
3. Did you bring your receipt with you?
   a ☐ bring   b ☐ receipt
4. Where did you buy it?
   a ☐ Where   b ☐ buy
5. Could you wait a moment, please?
   a ☐ Could   b ☐ wait
6. Can you take our order now, please?
   a ☐ take   b ☐ order
7. Can I change these jeans for another pair?
   a ☐ Can   b ☐ change
8. Could you call the manager, please?
   a ☐ call   b ☐ manager

10D Skills for Writing
We're really sorry we missed it

1 READING

a Read the three emails and tick (✓) the correct answers.

	Email A	Email B	Email C
1 Which email is about changing the date of a meeting?	☐	☐	☐
2 Which email is about some problems with a family holiday?	☐	☐	☐
3 Which email is from the parents of a very young child who was ill?	☐	☐	☐

Email A

Dear Mr Patterson

Thank you for your email of 5 September about the problems you had during your holiday with Turkish Sun Tours. I am writing to apologise for putting you in a different hotel from your friends. Unfortunately, our agents in Turkey made a mistake with your booking and did not reserve enough rooms at the Hotel Paradise. This is why they had to put your family in another hotel in the same resort.

I hope you will book a holiday with us again in the future and we would like to offer you a 25% discount on your next holiday with us. This is our way of apologising for the problems you had.

Yours sincerely,

Pam Webster

Customer Services Manager, Turkish Sun Tours

Email B

Hi Jim

Just a quick message to say sorry that we couldn't come to your house for dinner last Saturday. Unfortunately, our youngest son, Jack, had a really high temperature, so we couldn't leave him with our babysitter.

Some friends of ours are coming round for lunch next Sunday so, if you're free, maybe you and Sarah could join us? Let me know if you can come. Hope to see you on Sunday.

Love

Melanie x

Email C

Dear Malcolm

I'm writing to let you know that I need to rearrange my trip to New York planned for next week. David Smith, our new Managing Director, has just asked me to go with him to Beijing on Sunday to attend a meeting with our Chinese distributor. I'm very sorry to cancel my trip at the last minute, but the meeting in China is really important.

Could we hold a meeting in New York during the week of 15 May instead? Let me know if you're free to meet that week.

Best wishes,

Amanda

b Read the three emails again. Are the sentences true or false?

1 Mr Patterson didn't stay in the same hotel as his friends.
2 The agents in Turkey couldn't find a hotel for Mr Patterson's family.
3 Turkish Sun Tours is going to give Mr Patterson a free holiday.
4 Melanie would like to invite Jim and Sarah to lunch next Sunday.
5 Amanda wants to meet Malcolm in Beijing next week.

2 WRITING SKILLS
Formal and informal language

a Read the sentences from an email from the manager of a restaurant to an unhappy customer. Rewrite the sentences and change the words in **bold** to make the email more formal.

1 **Hi** Mrs Miller
   Dear Mrs Miller
2 **Thanks** very much for your email of 15 June.
3 **I'm** writing to **say sorry** for the poor service you received in our restaurant last Saturday.
4 **We've** just opened the restaurant and **we've** had a few problems finding experienced waiters and waitresses.
5 However, **we're** working hard to improve our levels of service and **I'm** confident that we **won't** have any more problems of this kind in the future.
6 We hope **you'll** come back to our restaurant again and **we'd** like to offer you a 50% discount on your next meal with us.
7 This is our way of **saying sorry** for the problems **you've** had.
8 **Best wishes,**

3 WRITING

a Read the letter from David Hurst to a hotel in Sorrento. Write an email of apology from the manager of the hotel. Use the notes to help you.

10th July 2015

Dear Sir/Madam

Re: Problems at the Hotel Dante

I am writing to complain about the poor service I received when I stayed at your hotel in Sorrento last week.

First, when I booked the room on the Internet I asked for a room with a view of the sea. However, I was given a room with a view of the car park. Secondly, the receptionist was very rude to my wife when she had a problem with the shower. In fact, there wasn't enough hot water for us to have a shower for the first two days of our stay. Finally, the service in the restaurant was too slow. Every morning we had to wait at least half an hour for our breakfast.

I look forward to hearing from you.

Yours faithfully

David Hurst

Notes for reply to Mr Hurst
- apologise for poor service
- wrong room: problems with website?
- shower: problems with water heating system
- slow service in restaurant: three waiters ill that week
- offer a 50% discount on next visit?

61

UNIT 10
Reading and listening extension

1 READING

a Read the magazine article. Match the people 1–3 with the phrases a–c.

1 Isabella — b concentrate better
2 Jung-ho — c more relaxed
3 Caitlin — a too difficult

b Read the article again and tick (✓) the correct endings to the sentences.

1 In the magazine article, three people were asked …
 a ☐ what they thought about smartphones and technology.
 b ✓ not to use their smartphone for a week.
 c ☐ to imagine a world without technology.

2 Isabella thought that she would …
 a ☐ not be involved with other people if she didn't have her phone.
 b ☐ break up with her boyfriend if she didn't have her phone.
 c ☐ enjoy not having to use her phone.

3 Isabella realised that …
 a ☐ she didn't have enough time to spend with her friends.
 b ☐ she thought less about what other people were doing when she didn't have her phone.
 c ☐ she wasn't talking to her friends enough.

4 If Jung-ho didn't have his phone, …
 a ☐ he thought there would be serious problems with his business.
 b ☐ he thought he would have to work in the evenings more.
 c ☐ he wouldn't be able to make decisions.

5 Caitlin didn't want to stop using her phone because …
 a ☐ she liked to use it to read about fashion.
 b ☐ she needed it for her job.
 c ☐ she was worried that people wouldn't call her.

c Read the article again and tick (✓) the correct people. Sometimes there is more than one possible answer.

1 Who had a better private life without a smartphone?
 a ✓ Isabella   b ✓ Jung-ho   c ☐ Caitlin
2 Who thought they wouldn't be able to look after something properly without their phone?
 a ☐ Isabella   b ☐ Jung-ho   c ☐ Caitlin
3 Who realised that they didn't have to do things immediately?
 a ☐ Isabella   b ☐ Jung-ho   c ☐ Caitlin
4 Who was right to be worried about not having a phone?
 a ☐ Isabella   b ☐ Jung-ho   c ☐ Caitlin
5 Who realised that their social life would continue without a phone?
 a ☐ Isabella   b ☐ Jung-ho   c ☐ Caitlin
6 Who learned something positive from the experiment?
 a ☐ Isabella   b ☐ Jung-ho   c ☐ Caitlin
7 Who didn't complete the experiment?
 a ☐ Isabella   b ☐ Jung-ho   c ☐ Caitlin
8 Who found not communicating was a problem for their work?
 a ☐ Isabella   b ☐ Jung-ho   c ☐ Caitlin

d Write about what you would do if you couldn't use your phone for a week.
- How would you communicate with friends?
- How would you feel?
- What would the advantages and disadvantages be?

Please turn off your phones

In the world today, over 1 billion (1,000,000,000) people own a smartphone, and over 80% of them say that they never switch it off. We use smartphones for everything, from making phone calls to being personal fitness trainers, and with over 9,000,000 apps available, it seems that there isn't too much that they can't do.

But imagine if you had to live without your smartphone for a week, what would you do?

We asked three users to try.

ISABELLA, 17, STUDENT, MADRID, SPAIN

If I didn't have my phone for a week, I wouldn't be able to live. It's too important to be without. That's what I thought. When I feel like chatting to my friends, I'll use my phone. I even broke up with my last boyfriend using my phone. Without it I wouldn't be able to join in with everything that's happening. But this week I actually enjoyed not having it. I could concentrate better, I wasn't too worried about what everyone was saying or doing and I spent more time actually talking to my friends.

JUNG-HO, 46, BUSINESSMAN, BUSAN, KOREA

I'm on my smartphone all day. If I couldn't use it for a week, I wouldn't be able to take care of my business. It would be a disaster. But it wasn't. I worked more effectively when I was in the office, I had more time to think about everything and in the evenings I was a lot more relaxed. I realised that I could put off making decisions until I was in the office. It's really changed how I work and I think the business is actually doing better now.

CAITLIN, 24, FASHION WRITER, NEW YORK CITY, USA

I write a fashion blog. If I couldn't use my phone, I wouldn't have a job. It's what I do and who I am. When I find out something, I need to pass it on, quickly. That's why people read my blog. I tried it for a day. But it was too difficult. I couldn't take any photos of cool people on the streets or quickly add something to my blog when I was out at a party. I just wasn't doing enough. It was horrible.

2 LISTENING

a ▶10.6 Listen to the conversation and underline the people who said these things.

1 Buying something in a shop is usually more expensive than buying online.
   Zuza / Haluk / No one
2 When you buy online you can't get what you buy straight away.
   Zuza / Haluk / No one
3 Buying clothes can be difficult because you cannot try them on before you buy them.
   Zuza / Haluk / No one
4 You cannot return something that you buy online.
   Zuza / Haluk / No one
5 There are sometimes problems with the delivery of things you buy online.
   Zuza / Haluk / No one
6 If people stopped going to shops, they would all close.
   Zuza / Haluk / No one

b ▶10.6 Listen to the conversation again and tick (✓) the correct endings to the sentences.

1 Haluk thinks online shopping is better because …
   a ✓ you can buy things at any time of the day and it is often cheaper.
   b ☐ you don't have to leave your house and it is often cheaper.
   c ☐ you don't have to wait more than a few days and it is cheaper.
2 The coat that Haluk bought recently was …
   a ☐ damaged in the post.
   b ☐ too big for him.
   c ☐ the wrong size and colour.
3 The company who sold the coat …
   a ☐ has given him an explanation of what happened.
   b ☐ has given him a refund.
   c ☐ hasn't replied to his email.
4 Haluk buys books online because …
   a ☐ he doesn't like going to bookshops.
   b ☐ he can find more books online than in the bookshop.
   c ☐ the bookshop in his town has closed.
5 Zuza thinks that online shopping …
   a ☐ will have an effect on shops in the future.
   b ☐ has already had an effect on shops in her town.
   c ☐ is more fun than normal shopping.
6 Which of the statements is not true?
   a ☐ Zuza hopes that she will find love when she is shopping.
   b ☐ Zuza thinks that Haluk should stop buying things online.
   c ☐ Zuza thinks that Haluk will meet someone while he is at home.

c Write about the advantages and disadvantages of shopping online. Include answers to these questions:
   • What have you bought online?
   • Why did you buy it online?
   • Did you have any problems buying it online?

Review and extension

1 GRAMMAR

Correct the sentences.

1 This table isn't enough big for twenty people.
   This table isn't big enough for twenty people.
2 He invited too much people to his party – over 100!
3 If I would have a motorbike, I wouldn't take the bus to work.
4 This morning it was too cold for swim in the sea.
5 I will go on a diet if I were overweight.
6 If Chile would win the World Cup, he would be delighted.

2 VOCABULARY

Correct the sentences.

1 Could you look at my cat while I'm on holiday?
   Could you look after my cat while I'm on holiday?
2 Tim isn't here at the moment, but I can pass a message.
3 There's a very small menu in that restaurant, so the choose of food is very limited.
4 It's sad that Anna and Steven have broken down after being together for ten years.
5 If you aren't happy with your hotel, you should complain.
6 She was offered a better job, but turned it off.

3 WORDPOWER
Multi-word verbs with *on*

Underline the correct words to complete the sentences.

1 He *got* / *tried* / *kept* on the shoes, but they were too big.
2 I can't *go* / *put* / *get* on working so much – I'm exhausted!
3 It was quite dark in the restaurant, so I had to *get* / *carry* / *put* on my glasses to read the menu.
4 I'm not sleeping well because my neighbour's dog *puts* / *keeps* / *tries* on barking all night long.
5 It was a really cold day, so she decided to *put* / *try* / *carry* on her scarf and gloves.
6 Although it started raining, we decided to *put* / *try* / *carry* on playing tennis for another 20 minutes.
7 He went back to his bedroom and *tried* / *got* / *put* on with his homework.
8 Although they were dirty, I *kept* / *put* / *went* my shoes on when I went into his house.

REVIEW YOUR PROGRESS

Look again at Review your progress on p.106 of the Student's Book. How well can you do these things now?

3 = very well   2 = well   1 = not so well

I CAN …

talk about moral dilemmas	☐
describe problems with goods and services	☐
return goods and make complaints	☐
write an apology email.	☐

63

11A It's a robot that looks like a human

1 GRAMMAR
Defining relative clauses

a Complete the sentences with *who*, *which* or *where*.

1 Charles Dickens was the English author __who__ wrote *Oliver Twist*.
2 The Louvre is the museum in Paris _____ you can see the famous *Mona Lisa* by Leonardo da Vinci.
3 Last night we watched a TV programme _____ explained the causes of the First World War.
4 When I was on holiday, I met a man _____ worked for the BBC in Manchester.
5 This is the place in New Zealand _____ they made the film *The Lord of the Rings*.
6 Tim Berners-Lee was the scientist _____ invented the World Wide Web in the early 1990s.
7 That's the cash machine _____ gives you money in pounds or euros.
8 Near where I work, there's a gym _____ only costs £20 per month.
9 He knows a restaurant near the station _____ you can have a delicious three-course meal for only £15.
10 Maria's got an aunt in the USA _____ has been married four times!

b Correct the sentences.

1 There are some lovely boots in that shop who only cost £35!
   There are some lovely boots in that shop which only cost £35!
   OR
   There are some lovely boots in that shop that only cost £35!
2 There's a woman over there which used to work for your company.
   _____
3 There's a café near me it has 50 different kinds of tea!
   _____
4 My dad's got a cousin in Houston he works for NASA.
   _____
5 I know an Italian restaurant in London that you can have chocolate spaghetti!
   _____
6 I've got a new camera who also takes video pictures.
   _____
7 That's a cinema where they're showing the new James Bond film next week.
   _____
8 He's just bought a new TV it gives you access to the Internet.
   _____

2 VOCABULARY Compound nouns

a Complete the crossword puzzle.

→ **Across**

2 I bought my boots from the new s_hoe_ s_hop_ opposite the café.
4 British people usually put a t_____ b_____ in a cup with boiling water and milk to make their favourite hot drink.
6 The s_____ lights are turned on automatically when it starts getting dark.
10 There's a big c_____ p_____ near the city centre – it's got 750 spaces!
11 Mick Jagger is a famous r_____ s_____ who sings with The Rolling Stones.
12 If you want a really good choice of shops, you should go to the new shopping c_____ near the motorway.

↓ **Down**

1 Can you get me six c_____ cups from the cupboard, please? None of my friends drink tea.
3 The cinema's going to be full! Look at that long queue at the t_____ office.
5 I'm sure I wrote down her telephone number in my a_____ book.
7 While they were carrying the new TV into the house, they dropped it and broke the T_____ s_____.
8 I couldn't get any money out because the cash m_____ wasn't working.
9 When he's finished his homework, he usually plays computer g_____ for an hour before dinner.

3 PRONUNCIATION
Word stress: compound nouns

a 🔊 11.1 Listen to the compound nouns and underline the main stressed syllable.

1 <u>mountain</u> climbing
2 computer screen
3 science fiction
4 address book
5 bread knife
6 car park
7 coffee cup
8 bookshelf

64

11B I think they discovered it by chance

1 GRAMMAR Articles

a Complete the conversation at a tourist office with the correct articles: *a*, *an*, *the* or Ø.

A Good morning. Please take ¹_*a*_ seat. I'll be with you in ²_____ moment … Now, how can I help you?

B Could you help us to find ³_____ hotel in ⁴_____ London, please?

A Yes, of course. Would you like ⁵_____ hotel in the city centre?

B Yes, if possible.

A OK, how about ⁶_____ Hotel Stella? They've got some rooms free.

B Is it near ⁷_____ underground station?

A Yes, it is. It's about five minutes' walk from ⁸_____ Marble Arch station. And it's very close to ⁹_____ Hyde Park. It's one of ¹⁰_____ nicest hotels in London.

B Great. Can you ask if they have ¹¹_____ double room for three nights? And can you check ¹²_____ price?

A Yes, sure. I'm afraid ¹³_____ hotels in London are really expensive. A lot of ¹⁴_____ people think that London's ¹⁵_____ most expensive city for ¹⁶_____ tourists in ¹⁷_____ world.

B Yes, ¹⁸_____ hotel that we stayed in last year cost over £200 a night!

A Right, I've booked it for you. When you come out of ¹⁹_____ underground station, go along ²⁰_____ Edgware Road for about 200 metres and it's on ²¹_____ right, opposite ²²_____ cinema.

B Brilliant. Thanks very much.

b ▶11.2 Listen and check.

c Correct the sentences.
1 That film was most exciting thriller I've ever seen.
   That film was the most exciting thriller I've ever seen.
2 In the UK, the police officers don't usually carry guns.
3 I love the Italian ice cream. It's the best in the world!
4 They drove to Paris by car and then stayed in the lovely hotel near the Eiffel Tower.
5 France is the most popular country for the tourists in the world.
6 Doctors in USA are paid much more than nurses.

2 VOCABULARY
Adverbials: luck and chance

a Match 1–8 with a–h to make sentences.
1 [f] I didn't have enough money to pay the taxi driver, but fortunately,
2 [ ] He didn't train very hard for his first marathon, but amazingly,
3 [ ] Look, I didn't break your phone on purpose. I
4 [ ] While they were moving the furniture around, they accidentally
5 [ ] The president was very popular so, as expected,
6 [ ] We got to the airport on time, but unfortunately,
7 [ ] My grandmother fell over again yesterday, but luckily,
8 [ ] I found these old letters from my uncle by chance

a accidentally dropped it while I was getting out of the car.
b he won the election very easily with 75% of the vote.
c while I was fixing the old desk in my aunt's bedroom.
d broke my computer screen.
e our flight to Moscow was delayed because of the storms.
f my friend had five euros to lend me.
g he finished it in just less than three hours.
h she didn't break her arm this time.

b <u>Underline</u> the correct words to complete the sentences.
1 *Surprisingly* / *As expected*, Real Madrid beat the third division team very easily, winning 6 – 0.
2 *Luckily* / *Unfortunately*, I've lost my front door key, so I can't get into my house.
3 The ruins of the ancient city were discovered completely *by chance* / *on purpose* while the construction company were building the new motorway.
4 *Accidentally* / *Luckily*, it stopped raining in the afternoon, so we were able to take the children to the beach.
5 Sorry, but it was an accident. I didn't do it *on purpose* / *as expected*.
6 *Unfortunately* / *Amazingly*, although he didn't work very hard, he got 95% in his final exam!

3 PRONUNCIATION Stress in adverbials

a ▶11.3 Listen to the words and tick (✓) the stressed syllable in each word.
1 accidentally
  a ☐ ac   b ✓ den
2 on purpose
  a ☐ pur b ☐ pose
3 by chance
  a ☐ by   b ☐ chance
4 unfortunately
  a ☐ un   b ☐ for
5 luckily
  a ☐ luc b ☐ ly
6 surprisingly
  a ☐ sur b ☐ pri
7 amazingly
  a ☐ ma   b ☐ zing
8 fortunately
  a ☐ for b ☐ nate
9 as expected
  a ☐ ex   b ☐ pec

65

11C Everyday English
It's straight ahead

1 USEFUL LANGUAGE
Asking for and giving directions in a building

a ▶11.4 Listen and put the directions in the correct order.

Can you tell me where the Kensington Meeting Room is?
☐ Then go up the stairs to the first floor.
☐ The Kensington Room is the fourth door on the right.
☒1 Yes, sure. It's on the first floor.
☐ Then go down to the end of the corridor.
☐ At the top of the stairs, turn left along another corridor.
☐ Go through that door over there.
Great, thanks.

b ▶11.4 Listen again and check.

c Put the words in the correct order to make sentences.

1 the stairs / ground floor / the / to / go down .
   Go down the stairs to the ground floor.
2 go through / those / and then / doors / down / the corridor .
   _____
3 along / so, first / to the / go / stairs / the corridor ?
   _____
4 tell / where / the / you / is, please / staff restaurant / me / could ?
   _____
5 the right / the / down / and it's / the first / on / office / then go / corridor .
   _____
6 floor / go / the / to / stairs / the third / up .
   _____
7 can / check / so, / just / I ?
   _____
8 I've / right, / think / that / I / got .
   _____
9 corridor / the top of / the / go / another / right and / stairs, / turn / along / at .
   _____
10 the meeting room / is / second / left / on / the / door / the .
   _____

d ▶11.5 Listen and check.

2 PRONUNCIATION
Sound and spelling: /ɜː/ and /ɔː/

a ▶11.6 Listen to the words. Tick (✓) the word you hear from each pair.

	/ɜː/		/ɔː/
1	☐ bird	✓	bored
2	☐ fur	☐	four
3	☐ sir	☐	sore
4	☐ shirt	☐	short
5	☐ word	☐	ward
6	☐ earl	☐	all
7	☐ pearl	☐	Paul
8	☐ worm	☐	warm

11D Skills for Writing
In my opinion, it's because of the Internet

1 READING

a Read the web posts on the right and tick (✓) the correct answer.

- a ☐ Bicycles have always been very cheap to buy.
- b ☐ Cycling is a popular hobby for a lot of people.
- c ☐ Cycling is bad for the environment.
- d ☐ Streets with electric lighting were more dangerous.

b Read the web posts again. Are the sentences true or false?

1. It was cheaper to have a bicycle than to travel on public transport.
2. Bicycles are not very popular in the developing world.
3. When lots of people cycle to work, cities become less polluted.
4. Gas lighting was invented after electric lighting.
5. Reading and writing at night was easier with electric lighting.

2 WRITING SKILLS
Expressing results and reasons

a Underline the correct words to complete the sentences.

1. *As a result of / As / Because* better windows, new houses lose less heat in winter and people spend less money on keeping them warm.
2. In the 1960s, people couldn't afford to go to the USA on holiday *because of / as / as a result of* air travel was so expensive.
3. People didn't use their mobile phones when they were travelling abroad *as a result of / because of / because* phone calls were so expensive.
4. Computers are much smaller now *as / because / because of* the invention of the micro-chip.
5. *As / As a result of / Because of* you can travel by train from London to Paris in less than three hours now, I won't need to catch the plane any more.
6. Nowadays, malaria is less common in Africa *as / as a result of / because* the new vaccination programme.
7. *Because / As / Because of* the terrible pollution, many European cities only allow people to drive their cars on certain days of the month.
8. She decided to buy a tablet *because of / because / as a result of* it was much easier to carry around than her old laptop.

The bicycle was invented in the 19th century. At first, bicycles were very expensive, but at the beginning of the 20th century, they were mass-produced in large factories. As a result of this, they became much cheaper and after that, most people could afford to buy one. Bicycles changed the way people travelled short distances. Because of the bicycle, people who didn't have much money didn't have to travel to work on buses or trains. As a result, they saved money and could get a job further away from where they lived. Today, bicycles are the most important form of transport for people in many countries in the developing world. Cycling is also a very popular sporting activity for many people, as it is a great way to stay fit and healthy. In big cities, a lot of people cycle to work and this helps to reduce pollution and protect the environment. Because of this, it seems to me that the bicycle is one of the most important inventions of the last 200 years.

Martin Roberts

In my opinion, the most important invention is the electric light. The electric light bulb was invented in the 19th century and slowly replaced gas lighting in the streets of big cities and in people's homes. With electric lights, the streets of big cities became safer and, as a result, there was less crime. Also, electric light bulbs improved the lighting in people's houses. As a result, they could do more things when it got dark in the evenings, such as reading books or writing letters. Electric lights have greatly improved the quality of people's lives and it is hard to imagine life without them.

Naomi Stevens

3 WRITING

a Write a web post about the invention of mobile phones. Use the notes to help you.

Notes for web post about mobile phones
- most important invention = mobile phone
- before: had to be home, office or public phone box
- keep in contact with friends, family, colleagues
- speak wherever you are: street, supermarket, car, train
- stay in touch with children + elderly relatives
- useful if accident or to call the police
- not only calls and texts: also photos, videos, music, Internet, Facebook
- my phone = my most useful possession: where would I be without it?

67

UNIT 11
Reading and listening extension

1 READING

a Read the story and complete the sentences.
1 Juliane and her ___mother___ took a flight from Lima to Pucallpa.
2 The _____ was hit by lightning.
3 The plane crashed in the _____.
4 Juliane found some _____ to eat.
5 Juliane followed a small _____ through the forest.
6 Some men found Juliane and took her down the river in a _____.
7 A small aeroplane flew her to the _____ in Pucallpa.

b Read the story again. Are the sentences true or false?
1 Juliane was the only person who did not die in the crash.
2 The food that she found belonged to the other passengers.
3 Juliane was not prepared for life in the rainforest.
4 There were people in the hut that Juliane found.
5 The men who found Juliane had a small aeroplane.

c Read the story again. Match 1–6 with a–f to make sentences.

1 The flight which
2 The bone that
3 The lessons that
4 The boat which
5 The men who
6 The hospital where

a found Juliane took her down the river.
b Juliane broke was in her neck.
c Juliane found belonged to the men who helped her.
d Juliane was on crashed in the rainforest.
e Juliane's father taught her helped her survive.
f Juliane was taken was in Pucallpa.

d Imagine you are Juliane. Write a letter to a friend explaining your experience in the forest. Remember to include:
- what happened to you
- how you felt at the time
- how you feel now.

Amazing but true

There are many true stories about people who have been in a plane crash but didn't die, but what happened to Juliane Koepcke is one of the most amazing stories.

Juliane and her parents lived in Peru. On Christmas Eve in 1971, 17-year-old Juliane was on a plane that was flying from Lima to Pucallpa in Peru with her mother, Maria. They were travelling to meet Juliane's father, who was working in Pucallpa.

Unfortunately, the plane never arrived. During the flight, it was hit by lightning and broke up above the rainforest. Juliane fell over 3,000 metres to the ground and landed still in her seat, and amazingly, still alive. Everyone else on board died. Juliane had a broken bone in her neck and cuts to her arms, but surprisingly, she could still walk.

First of all, she tried to find her mother. Unfortunately, she couldn't see her so decided to look for some food instead. Luckily, she found some sweets which passengers had taken with them for the Christmas holidays. This was the only food that she found to eat.

Juliane's father was a biologist who had spent a lot of time in the rainforests in Peru with his family. Fortunately, he had taught Juliane some important lessons in how to stay alive. The skills that Juliane had learnt helped her in the rainforest. When she found a small river, she knew that if she followed it, it would take her to a village. It also gave her fresh water to drink and a natural path through the forest.

She walked and swam for nine days until, as expected, she found an empty hut made of wood. By chance, she also found a boat. Juliane wanted to leave but she didn't want to take the boat because it wasn't hers. So she waited. Luckily, hours later the men who used the hut came back and found Juliane. They helped to look after her and the next day took her in the boat down the river to a place where there was a small aeroplane which could take her to the hospital in Pucallpa. No one really knows why Juliane lived and everyone else died on the flight, but everyone agrees that it is an amazing story.

Review and extension

1 GRAMMAR

Correct the sentences.

1 *Rocky* was the film what Sylvester Stallone made in 1976.
  Rocky was the film that Sylvester Stallone made in 1976.
2 Sorry, I can't talk to you right now because I'm at the work.
3 Generally speaking, most the men like watching sport on TV.
4 Modern Living is the shop who I bought my leather sofa.
5 Look! That's a man who stole my wallet!
6 John F. Kennedy was the American president which was assassinated in Dallas in 1963.

2 VOCABULARY

Correct the sentences.

1 They're having a sale at the shoes shop next to the cinema.
  They're having a sale at the shoe shop next to the cinema.
2 I think I wrote his phone number in my book address.
3 Surprisedly, it tasted a bit like chicken.
4 I'm afraid of heights, so I don't want to go rockclimbing.
5 He opened the car's door without looking and hit an old man on a bicycle.
6 I'm sorry I broke your cup of coffee – it was an accident.

3 WORDPOWER Preposition + noun

Match 1–6 with a–f to make sentences.

1 [f] Their plane didn't leave on
2 [ ] My parents are still in
3 [ ] I didn't break your glasses on
4 [ ] All of the bank robbers are now in
5 [ ] There are lots of tablets for
6 [ ] Next time you come to London, tell me in

a love with each other after 30 years of marriage.
b sale on eBay. I might get one.
c advance so I can book some theatre tickets.
d prison, apart from the one who escaped.
e purpose. I sat on them by mistake.
f time. It was 30 minutes late.

REVIEW YOUR PROGRESS

Look again at Review your progress on p.116 of the Student's Book. How well can you do these things now?
3 = very well   2 = well   1 = not so well

I CAN ...

explain what technology does	☐
describe how discoveries were made	☐
ask for and give directions in a building	☐
write a post expressing an opinion.	☐

2 LISTENING

a ▶11.7 Listen to the conversation. Number the events in the correct order.

☐ The police arrived.
☐ The car with one man inside drove into the cash machine.
☐ The men drove the car into something in the street.
☐ The men ran away into a park.
☐ The men took some money from the machine.
☐ The men tried to break open the cash machine.
[1] A car with two men inside drove into the cash machine very fast.

b ▶11.7 Listen to the conversation again and tick (✓) the correct answers.

1 Where was Margaret Edwards when the vehicle crashed into the cash machine?
  a ☐ In the bedroom.
  b ☐ In the bathroom.
  c ✓ In another room.
2 At first, Margaret thought the crash was ...
  a ☐ an accident.
  b ☐ amazing.
  c ☐ done on purpose.
3 What did the men use to try and break open the machine?
  a ☐ Something they found in the street.
  b ☐ Something they were wearing.
  c ☐ Something that was in the car.
4 One of the men ...
  a ☐ was wearing dark glasses.
  b ☐ looked like a baseball player.
  c ☐ was much older than the other man.
5 What happened when they opened the cash machine?
  a ☐ They were able to take a lot of money.
  b ☐ The police came.
  c ☐ The men decided to run away.
6 Why didn't the men drive away?
  a ☐ Because they didn't have the key to the car.
  b ☐ Because the car was damaged.
  c ☐ Because the police stopped them.

c Write about a surprising or amazing thing you may have seen. Remember to include:
• what you saw
• what happened
• how you felt.

69

12A I had always thought they were dangerous

1 VOCABULARY Animals

a Complete the crossword puzzle.

→ **Across**
3 This insect bites humans and drinks their blood. _mosquito_
5 This animal lives in deserts and can travel long distances without food or water. _____
6 This insect produces honey. _____
7 This bird is large, very colourful and can learn to 'talk' by copying what someone says to it. _____

↓ **Down**
1 This animal has eight legs and makes webs to catch small flies. One of the biggest kinds is the tarantula. _____
2 This animal is the largest kind of monkey in the world. _____
4 The blue _____ is the biggest animal on the planet.
8 This is the largest animal of the cat family and is orange with black stripes. _____

2 GRAMMAR Past perfect

a Complete the sentences with the past perfect forms of the verbs in the box.

| steal work get up miss stop ~~leave~~ begin finish |

1 By the time we got to the station, my sister's train _had_ already _left_.
2 When my grandmother phoned, I _____ just _____ doing my homework.
3 He _____ really hard at school all year, so he got excellent marks in his exams.
4 Anthony arrived late for school this morning because he _____ late.
5 When they got to the cinema, the film _____ just _____.
6 When he got back from holiday, he found that someone _____ his car.
7 We had to take a taxi home from the station because we _____ the last bus.
8 The two men _____ arguing by the time the police arrived.

b Complete the text with the past simple or past perfect forms of the verbs in brackets.

We ¹ _had_ (have) a terrible journey on the way to Barcelona. The problems ² _____ (begin) when we ³ _____ (leave) home at 6.30 in the morning. There ⁴ _____ (be) a huge traffic jam on the motorway because two lorries ⁵ _____ (crash) and the road ⁶ _____ (be) completely blocked. By the time we ⁷ _____ (reach) the airport, we ⁸ _____ (miss) our flight. It ⁹ _____ (take) off five minutes before we ¹⁰ _____ (arrive) at the check-in desk. We ¹¹ _____ (try) to buy some tickets for the next flight to Barcelona, but they ¹² _____ (sell) all the seats. In the end, we ¹³ _____ (buy) tickets for a flight at 7 o'clock that evening and ¹⁴ _____ (spend) the whole day at the airport. We ¹⁵ _____ (land) in Barcelona at 21:45, but we ¹⁶ _____ (not collect) our suitcases from the arrivals hall until 11 o'clock because there ¹⁷ _____ (be) a baggage handlers' strike that day. By the time our taxi driver ¹⁸ _____ (find) our hotel, the restaurant ¹⁹ _____ (close), so we ²⁰ _____ (go) straight to bed without having dinner.

3 PRONUNCIATION
Sound and spelling: /ʌ/, /ɔː/ and /əʊ/

a ▶12.1 Look at the words and listen to the pronunciation of the letters in **bold**. Complete the table with the words in the box.

| ~~br**ough**t~~ c**o**me d**o**ne f**a**llen kn**ow**n sp**o**ken r**u**n t**augh**t w**o**ken w**o**n |

Sound 1 /ʌ/ (e.g. dr**u**nk)	Sound 2 /ɔː/ (e.g. b**ough**t)	Sound 3 /əʊ/ (e.g. ch**o**sen)
	brought	

70

12B He said I was selfish!

1 GRAMMAR Reported speech

a Underline the correct words to complete the sentences.

1. Matthew said, 'I want to play football with my friends.'
   He *told me / said me / told* that *we want / I wanted / he wanted* to play football with *my / his / your* friends.
2. Naomi said, 'I'll help you with the washing-up.'
   She *told / said / said me* that *she will / I would / she would* help *me / her / you* with the washing-up.
3. Angela said, 'My mum's watching a film on TV with my little brother.'
   She *told / told me / said me* that *my / his / her* mum *had watched / was watching / watching* a film on TV with *her / his / my* little brother.
4. David said, 'We went to the park with some friends from our school.'
   He *said / told / said me* that *they've been / they'd been / we've been* to the park with some friends from *our / her / their* school.
5. James said, 'Andy, my dad can't take us to the zoo on Saturday.'
   He *said me / told him / said him* that *my / her / his* dad *couldn't / could / didn't can* take *us / them / me* to the zoo on Saturday.
6. Josh said, 'I think that we'll go to the beach with our cousins after lunch.'
   He *told / told us / said us* that he *is thinking / thought / had thought* that *we will go / he would go / they would go* to the beach with *my / their / her* cousins after lunch.
7. She said, 'I've already done all my homework.'
   She *said / told / said me* that *she already did / I've already done / she'd already done* all *my / his / her* homework.
8. Adam said, 'My little sister isn't going to come to my birthday party!'
   He *told / told us / said us* that *my / her / his* little sister *isn't going to / wasn't going to / not going to* come to *his / her / our* birthday party.

b Read the direct speech sentences. Use reported speech to report what the speaker said. Make any necessary changes to the highlighted words.

1. 'I'm waiting for my bus to come.'
   She said she was waiting for her bus to come. OR She said that she was waiting for her bus to come.
2. 'I'll invite you and your brother to my house for dinner next week.'
   He told me …
3. 'You can use my tablet to do your homework.'
   She told James …
4. 'The traffic was really bad, so we missed the 17:15 train.'
   He said …
5. 'We're going to buy you a lovely present for your birthday.'
   She told me …
6. 'I've just tried calling my friend, but she didn't reply, so I think she's away on holiday.'
   He said …

2 VOCABULARY Personality adjectives

a Complete the crossword puzzle.

2 across: HONEST

→ **Across**

2. He's so __honest__! When a shop assistant gave him too much change yesterday he didn't keep it – he told her she'd made a mistake.
5. She's extremely _____ – she's got lots of friends and she loves meeting new people.
7. You know, I've never seen Jim laugh and he rarely smiles – he's always so _____.
8. She's really _____ – she hates having to talk to people she doesn't know at parties.
10. He's a very _____ person – he worries about everything.

↓ **Down**

1. You're so _____! That's the second time you've lost your house keys this month.
3. You're so _____ – why should we always do what you want to do? Why can't you think about other people for a change?
4. She's a very _____ person. Although she hasn't got much money, she bought all her friends dinner when it was her birthday.
6. He's a very _____ person – he writes poems and short stories and loves painting.
9. Mike's a really _____ guy – he's always telling us jokes and making us laugh.

3 PRONUNCIATION Word stress

a ▶12.2 Listen to the words and tick (✓) the stressed syllable in each word.

		a	b
1	careless	✓ care	less
2	serious	se	ous
3	selfish	sel	fish
4	easy going	ea	go
5	reliable	re	li
6	confident	con	dent
7	patient	pa	tient
8	anxious	an	xious
9	generous	gen	rous
10	creative	cre	a

71

12C Everyday English
I'm pretty sure it's Japanese

1 USEFUL LANGUAGE
Agreeing and disagreeing

a Match 1–8 with a–h to make sentences.

1. [g] I believe yoga is a great way to relax before you go to bed.
2. [ ] I think Brazil have the best football team in the world.
3. [ ] In my opinion, Venice is a more attractive city than Florence.
4. [ ] This is a nicer cinema than the one we went to last week.
5. [ ] Barcelona is the biggest city in Spain.
6. [ ] Leonardo DiCaprio is a better actor than Brad Pitt.
7. [ ] In my view, Italian coffee is better than French coffee.
8. [ ] I think the weather in the UK in winter is much better than in Germany.

a I don't think so. I think there are more people in Madrid, actually.
b That's true. He was brilliant in *The Great Gatsby*.
c I agree. The seats are very comfortable and the screen is wider.
d I'm not sure about that. I think Argentina will beat them in the final.
e Definitely. It's such a beautiful place to visit. I love it!
f I'm afraid I don't agree. Here it rains so much in January and February. I can't stand it!
g You're absolutely right. I try and do a few exercises every night.
h I'm sorry, but how do you know? You don't drink coffee!

b ▶12.3 Listen and check.

c Underline the correct words to complete the exchanges.

1. **A** I think the Amazon is the longest river in the world.
   B *Definitely. / I don't think so. / That's true.* Actually, I think the Nile is longer than the Amazon.
2. **A** Swiss chocolate is much nicer than British chocolate.
   B *You're absolutely right. / Oh, please. / I'm not sure about that.* It's probably the best in the world.
3. **A** Russian is a harder language to learn than Spanish.
   B *Oh, please. / I don't think so. / Definitely.* In my view, Spanish is one of the easiest languages to learn.
4. **A** Everybody should retire when they reach sixty.
   B *That's right. / Oh, please. / Exactly.* That's much too early! Older people have so much experience which they can pass on to their younger colleagues.
5. **A** Tablets are so much more practical than laptops.
   B *I'm sorry, but I don't agree. / I'm afraid you're wrong. / That's true.* They're much lighter and easier to carry.
6. **A** His last film was brilliant!
   B *I'm not sure about that. / You're right. / I don't think so.* It's the best film he's made so far.

d ▶12.4 Listen and check.

2 PRONUNCIATION Main stress: contrastive

a ▶12.5 Listen to the exchanges and tick (✓) the stressed word in each of B's responses.

		Stressed word
1	**A** Antonio Banderas is a Mexican actor. **B** Er, he's actually a Spanish actor.	Spanish ✓ actor
2	**A** French food's the best in the world. **B** Well, actually, I think Italian food is the best.	Italian food
3	**A** I like the American English accent. **B** Do you? I prefer British English, actually.	British English
4	**A** New York's the best place to live in the USA. **B** Actually, I think San Francisco's the best place.	San Francisco best
5	**A** I think Chelsea will win the Champions League this year. **B** No way! Barcelona will win it this year.	Barcelona win
6	**A** Baseball is the most popular sport in the USA. **B** I'm sorry, but I think American football is the most popular sport.	American football sport

12D Skills for Writing
About an hour later, the rain stopped

1 READING

a Read the text on the right and tick (✓) the correct answer.

- a ☐ The old lady lost her handbag in the park.
- b ☐ The thief gave the handbag back to the old lady.
- c ☐ The police officers thought Tom had stolen a handbag.
- d ☐ Tom stopped a man who had taken a woman's handbag.

b Read the text again. Are the sentences true or false?

1. Tom was walking across the park with Brian when he heard the old lady.
2. The young man couldn't escape because Tom was sitting on him.
3. Both police officers asked Tom to explain what had happened.
4. Tom didn't want to accept the old lady's money at first.
5. The old lady didn't have much money.

2 WRITING SKILLS
Linkers: past time

a Underline the correct words to complete the sentences.

1. *As soon as* / *Suddenly* the police arrived, the man started running down the street.
2. He saw the strange man with the black dog at 7:30 in the morning. *Suddenly* / *Later that day*, he saw him again, but this time without his dog.
3. They said goodnight and went back to their hotel to sleep. *As soon as* / *The following morning*, they caught the train to Paris.
4. We were sitting outside a café, reading the guidebook. *After a while* / *Suddenly*, there was a huge explosion and people started running in all directions.
5. The sky was covered in dark clouds. *A few minutes later* / *Later that year*, it started to rain very heavily.

Local hero

One hot day last July, Tom was walking home from university after playing in a rugby match. He had just said goodbye to his best friend, Brian, and was walking across the park near his house. Suddenly, he heard someone shouting, 'Stop, thief!' He turned round and saw a little old lady. She was pointing at a young man of about 20 who was running towards him. 'He's stolen my handbag!' she shouted. The thief was coming towards Tom and the old lady shouted to him, 'Hey, you! Stop him!' A few seconds later, Tom threw himself at the young man and the thief fell over on the path. Tom immediately sat on the thief's back so he couldn't escape. A few minutes later Tom heard a siren and saw the flashing blue light of a police car. The old lady had called the police on her mobile phone and, luckily, a police car had been near the park at the time.

Two police officers got out of the car quickly and ran towards Tom and the thief as fast as they could. As soon as they got to Tom, they immediately arrested the young man. While one of them took him to the police car, the other started asking Tom and the old lady some questions about what had happened. Tom gave the old lady her handbag. Fortunately, everything was still inside it. The old lady thanked Tom and asked him for his telephone number. She explained that she couldn't stop because she was going to visit a friend in hospital. When the old lady had gone, Tom told the police officer what had happened and he wrote everything down in his notebook. Finally, he gave the police officer his phone number and went home.

The following day the old lady phoned Tom. She thanked him again and invited him to her house. She said that she wanted to give him a reward. Later that week Tom went to visit the old lady at her house. She lived in a big house near the park and there was a Rolls-Royce in front of it. While they talked she made him a cup of tea and gave him some delicious chocolate cake. Then, just as he was standing up to leave, she opened her handbag and gave him £500. Tom told her that he didn't want to take it, but she insisted: 'Please take it. I've got plenty of money and I'd really like to thank you for being so brave.' In the end Tom agreed to take it and used it to buy a new laptop.

3 WRITING

a David went on a walking holiday in Scotland last year. Write a story about what happened. Use the time expressions in the box and the notes to help you.

about an hour later   suddenly   after a while   later that day
10 minutes later   as soon as   the following day   later that evening
after a short time   soon   last year   when

Notes on accident during walking holiday

- Scotland + 3 friends
- accident – top of a mountain? eating sandwiches?
- weather changed – heavy snow – only see 20 metres
- started walking down path: next village (spend the night?)
- snow: getting deeper?
- all confident walkers: no problems?
- shout from behind me: Anthony lying on the ground (fallen over a rock?)
- leg hurting badly: broken?
- call for help? Mobile phone: emergency services
- mountain rescue team (helicopter)
- arrived hospital
- leg not badly broken: no need to operate – all felt v. relieved

UNIT 12
Reading and listening extension

We bought a zoo

In March 2005, Benjamin Mee received a letter from his sister. Inside was an advertisement for a house that was for sale. It was a house with a zoo full of animals in its garden.

Earlier that year, Benjamin's father had died and his mother was living alone in a large house in London, which she was trying to sell for £1.2 million, the same price as the zoo. Benjamin, who was living in France with his wife and two children, thought that it would be wonderful for his family to sell his mother's house and buy the zoo so that they could all live together and take care of each other. He knew that his father, a sensible man, would not have agreed. But Benjamin was thinking of the future.

Surprisingly, his family agreed. Benjamin's mother was very generous and happy to buy the zoo after selling her house. The year before she had spent a day at a zoo helping the zoo keepers and had really enjoyed looking after the animals. Benjamin's wife was more anxious. She was very ill and didn't want to change her life, but Benjamin said that it would help her and the children think about something else.

Unfortunately, buying the zoo was quite difficult, but Benjamin was patient and confident, and after a year of trying, in October 2006, they did it. But four days after the family moved into the zoo, there was a disaster. A jaguar, a large black cat, had escaped, after a zoo keeper had forgotten to close a door. The family also needed £500,000 for repairs before they could open it. Then while they were doing the repairs, Benjamin's wife died.

On 7 July 2007, the zoo opened and the first visitors came to see the animals. There were tigers, bears, monkeys, parrots, snakes and spiders, and lots of others. People loved the zoo, and loved what Benjamin, his children, who were always sociable and friendly with visitors, and his family had done.

In 2008, he wrote a book called *We bought a zoo*, which became very popular. A Hollywood producer read the story and decided to make a film about it, and in 2012, the film was released and the money Benjamin earned from it helped to pay the bills and keep the zoo open.

If you'd like to visit the zoo that Benjamin's family bought, it's called the Dartmoor Zoological Gardens, in south-west England.

1 READING

a Read the magazine article above. Put the events in the correct order.

- ☐ Benjamin and his family buy the zoo.
- ☐ 1 Benjamin's mother spends a day at a zoo.
- ☐ The zoo opens.
- ☐ Benjamin's father dies.
- ☐ A Hollywood film is made about the zoo.
- ☐ Benjamin receives a letter from his sister.

b Read the magazine article again. Match the adjectives and the descriptions with the people. Complete the table with the words in the boxes.

Adjectives	Descriptions
anxious	friendly with people
generous	gave lots of money to buy something
~~patient~~	~~waited a year to do something~~
sociable	was worried about changing something

	Adjective	Description
1 Benjamin	patient	waited a year to do something
2 Benjamin's wife		
3 Benjamin's mother		
4 Benjamin's children		

c Read the magazine article again. Tick (✓) the correct responses.

1 Why did Benjamin want to buy the zoo?
  a ☐ He had always wanted to work with animals.
  b ✓ He wanted to bring his family closer at a difficult time.
  c ☐ His mother was a zoo keeper.

2 How did the jaguar escape?
  a ☐ The zoo keeper hadn't done something that was important.
  b ☐ The zoo needed to be repaired.
  c ☐ A visitor opened the door.

3 Benjamin's wife died …
  a ☐ before Benjamin bought the zoo.
  b ☐ before the zoo opened.
  c ☐ when the zoo opened.

4 How did the Hollywood film help Benjamin and the zoo?
  a ☐ Lots of people visited the zoo after they saw the film.
  b ☐ Benjamin wrote a book about it.
  c ☐ The money he got helped to run the zoo.

d Write a paragraph about a trip that you have recently been on. Remember to include:
- where you went
- what you did
- what preparation you had to do before you went
- what you thought of the trip.

74

Review and extension

1 GRAMMAR

Correct the sentences.

1 By the time we got to his house, the party finished.
   By the time we got to his house, the party had finished.
2 I said her that she couldn't go to the beach by herself.
3 He told me that my mother has called earlier that day.
4 We told that her father wouldn't buy her a new computer.
5 Tom never rode a camel before, so he was rather nervous.
6 Our train has already left when we finally arrived at the station.

2 VOCABULARY

Correct the sentences.

1 I had a great time at your party on Saturday. It was really funny.
   I had a great time at your party on Saturday. It was really fun.
2 She's a really onest person. If shop assistants give her too much change, she always tells them.
3 He's very easygoing. I'm sure he won't mind if you bring your friend with you when you go to his house for dinner.
4 I'm not a very confidant person. For example, I don't like speaking when I'm in a meeting with a large group of people.
5 Teachers have to learn to be patent with their students because sometimes they don't learn things immediately.
6 Why are you always so carless! You've already lost your mobile phone twice this year!

3 WORDPOWER *age*

Underline the correct words to complete the sentences.

1 My father's 48 this year, so he's definitely *of middle age / middle aged / in the middle of age*.
2 *At your age / In your age / On your age*, I was working 12 hours a day in a factory.
3 It's really important for young people to save money for their *older age / old age / third age*.
4 They're sisters who are only 18 months *different of age / apart in age / age difference*.
5 I learned to read *at an early age / of early age / at young age* – I could read when I was only three.
6 He's *near my age / old like me / about my age* – we both went to university at the same time.

REVIEW YOUR PROGRESS

Look again at Review your progress on p.126 of the Student's Book. How well can you do these things now?
3 = very well   2 = well   1 = not so well

I CAN ...

tell a story	☐
talk about family relationships	☐
agree and disagree in discussions	☐
write a short story.	☐

2 LISTENING

a ▶12.6 Listen to the conversation. Put the events in the correct order.

☐ Brad goes back to the factory to collect the jewellery.
☐ Brad leaves the hostel with 10 dollars.
☒ 1 Brad meets two brothers in a tea house.
☐ Brad runs away and gets in a taxi.
☐ The brothers make Brad 30 necklaces.
☐ The brothers take Brad to a cash machine.
☐ The three men go sightseeing together.
☐ The two brothers take Brad to their jewellery factory.

b ▶12.6 Listen to the conversation again and read the sentences in direct speech. They are from Brad's story, but he uses reported speech. Tick (✓) the correct answers.

1 'We can take you to see some tigers tomorrow.'
   Who said this?
   a ☐ Brad   b ☐ Jay   c ✓ Viki
2 'I'll buy a small piece.'
   Who said this?
   a ☐ Brad   b ☐ Jay   c ☐ Viki
3 'It will be ready tomorrow.'
   What will be ready tomorrow?
   a ☐ the money
   b ☐ the jewellery
   c ☐ the hostel
4 'This is what you asked for yesterday.'
   What is *this*?
   a ☐ a small piece of jewellery
   b ☐ 30 necklaces
   c ☐ the money
5 'You will have to pay 100 dollars.'
   What for?
   a ☐ for the 30 necklaces
   b ☐ for the small piece of jewellery
   c ☐ for sightseeing
6 'I will take you to a cash machine.'
   Who said this?
   a ☐ Brad   b ☐ Jay   c ☐ Viki

c Write about a good or bad experience you've had on holiday. Remember to include:
- where you were
- what happened
- who you met.

Vox pop video

Unit 1: Communicating

1a ◀ Where do you usually meet new people?

a Watch video 1a and underline the correct words to complete the sentences.
1 Helen usually meets new people *through friends / at parties / on trains or buses*.
2 Ian usually meets new people *through cycling / through friends / at parties*.
3 Carla usually meets new people *at language classes or dance classes / through friends / through cycling*.
4 Jen usually meets new people *on trains or buses / at parties / at language classes or dance classes*.
5 Maria usually meets new people *on trains or buses / through cycling / through friends*.

1b ◀ What's a good first question to ask someone?

b Watch video 1b. Match 1–4 with a–d to make sentences.
1 [b] Helen's first question is usually about
2 [ ] Carla's first question is usually about
3 [ ] Jen's first question is usually about
4 [ ] Maria's first question is usually about

a the weather or where the person is from.
b something in the news or the weather.
c the person's hobbies.
d the person's free-time activities.

1c ◀ How do you keep in touch with your family?

c Watch video 1c and tick (✓) the correct answers.
1 Helen uses Skype or email to keep in touch with …
   a [ ] her parents.
   b [ ] her brother.
   c [✓] her son.
2 Ian usually communicates with his family …
   a [ ] by phone.
   b [ ] by letter.
   c [ ] on Facebook.
3 Maria keeps in touch with her family …
   a [ ] by letter.
   b [ ] on the Internet.
   c [ ] by text.
4 Carla contacts her family …
   a [ ] on her phone.
   b [ ] in person.
   c [ ] on her laptop.
5 Jen keeps in touch with her family by …
   a [ ] seeing them face to face.
   b [ ] sending them texts.
   c [ ] phoning them.
6 Maria communicates with her family …
   a [ ] face to face.
   b [ ] by phone.
   c [ ] on Facebook.

Unit 2: Travel

2a ◀ What was your last holiday like?

a Watch video 2a and tick (✓) the correct answers.
1 Jenny travelled around the USA by …
   a [ ] car.
   b [ ] train.
   c [✓] coach.
2 John spent his last holiday in …
   a [ ] London and Wales.
   b [ ] London and Scotland.
   c [ ] Scotland and Ireland.
3 Suzanne went to Mexico for …
   a [ ] one week.
   b [ ] two weeks.
   c [ ] three weeks.
4 For Rebecca's last holiday, she went to …
   a [ ] the USA.
   b [ ] South America.
   c [ ] Scotland.

2b ◀ Did you do any sightseeing?

b Watch video 2b and tick (✓) the correct answers.
1 Jenny visited …
   a [ ] New York and Boston.
   b [ ] Chicago and Los Angeles.
   c [✓] San Francisco and Las Vegas.
2 John visited …
   a [ ] Big Ben and the Houses of Parliament.
   b [ ] Buckingham Palace and Westminster Abbey.
   c [ ] the Tower of London and Big Ben.
3 When she was in Mexico, Suzanne …
   a [ ] did lots of sightseeing.
   b [ ] didn't do any sightseeing.
   c [ ] spent most of her time relaxing.
4 When she went to Chicago, Rebecca …
   a [ ] went on a bus tour.
   b [ ] saw the Hollywood sign.
   c [ ] didn't do much sightseeing.

Vox pop video

2c◀ Did you bring back any souvenirs?

c Watch video 2c. Match 1–4 with a–d to make sentences.

1. [d] When she went on her last holiday, Jenny
2. [ ] When he went on his last holiday, John
3. [ ] When she went on her last holiday, Suzanne
4. [ ] When she went on her last holiday, Rebecca

a didn't bring back any souvenirs.
b brought back lots of souvenirs.
c brought back some presents for his daughters.
d brought back a 'dream catcher'.

Unit 3: Money

3a◀ What three things have you bought recently?

a Watch video 3a. Complete the sentences with the names in the box.

Darren   Colin   ~~Lauren~~   Carolyn

1. _Lauren_ recently bought some food, some shoes and a magazine.
2. _____ recently bought some shoes, a T-shirt and a holiday.
3. _____ recently bought a dress, a fancy-dress costume and some bike lights.
4. _____ recently bought some spaghetti, some tomato sauce and a house.

3b◀ Is there anything you've bought in the last year but haven't used yet?

b Watch video 3b and underline the correct words to complete the sentences.

1. Lauren has some *shirts / shoes / jeans* she's never worn.
2. Carolyn bought a black dress *six months ago / last weekend / a year ago* in the sales.
3. Colin *never buys / doesn't usually buy / often buys* things he doesn't need.

3c◀ What are good ways to raise money for charity?

c Watch video 3c. Match the ideas for raising money 1–4 with the people who mentioned the ideas a–d.

1. [d] My favourite way of making money is to sell cakes to people.
2. [ ] A friend of mine raised money by cycling across Morocco.
3. [ ] You can cycle from London to Brighton to raise money for charity.
4. [ ] You can cut your hair really short to raise money for charity.

a Lauren
b Darren
c Colin
d Carolyn

Unit 4: Social Life

4a◀ What's the best party you've ever been to?

a Watch video 4a and tick (✓) the correct answers.

1. The best party Seb's ever been to was …
   a [ ] his brother's birthday party.
   b [ ] his school's Christmas party.
   c [✓] his friend's birthday party.
2. The best party Lucy's ever been to was …
   a [ ] her best friend's birthday party.
   b [ ] her own party.
   c [ ] her father's 50th birthday party.
3. The best party Wiktoria's ever been to was …
   a [ ] Simon's leaving party.
   b [ ] Simon's birthday party.
   c [ ] Simon's end-of-year party.
4. One of Solyman's favourite parties was when …
   a [ ] he was about 6.
   b [ ] he was about 16.
   c [ ] he was a student.

4b◀ What do you usually do to celebrate your birthday?

b Watch video 4b and underline the correct words to complete the sentences.

1. Last year Seb *had a party / did two special activities / went to a restaurant* with his friends.
2. Lucy usually has a *big party with all her friends / meal with her friends / meal with her family*.
3. Wiktoria usually has a *barbecue with her friends / barbecue with her family / party with her friends*.
4. Solyman *doesn't celebrate / always celebrates / sometimes celebrates* his birthday.

4c◀ What are your plans for the weekend?

c Watch video 4c. Match 1–4 with a–d to make sentences.

1. [b] This weekend Seb is
2. [ ] This weekend Lucy is
3. [ ] This weekend Wiktoria is
4. [ ] This weekend Solyman is

a doing some gardening.
b watching films with some friends.
c getting ready to go on holiday.
d going to London.

Unit 5: Work

5a ◄ Do you work?

a Watch video 5a and tick (✓) the correct answers.

1 Jen is a teacher of _____.
   a ☐ English
   b ☐ German
   c ✓ Russian

2 Christian shows _____ around Cambridge colleges.
   a ☐ teachers
   b ☐ tourists
   c ☐ students

3 Precious is working with children at a _____ school.
   a ☐ language
   b ☐ Sunday
   c ☐ summer

4 Helen visits _____ and clients two or three days a week.
   a ☐ hospitals
   b ☐ hostels
   c ☐ hotels

5b ◄ What qualifications or abilities are necessary for your job?

b Watch video 5b and underline the correct words to complete the sentences.

1 In Jen's job you need to be able to *write / speak / understand* the language you're teaching.
2 In Christian's job you have to be good at *listening to / working with / talking to* people.
3 In Precious's job you need to be very *friendly / funny / creative*.
4 People who do Helen's job often have a background in *engineering / computing / science*.

5c ◄ What do you think makes people happy at work?

c Watch video 5c. Match 1–4 with a–d to make sentences.

1 [b] Jen thinks that people like their jobs if
2 ☐ Christian thinks that people like their jobs if
3 ☐ Precious thinks that people like their jobs if
4 ☐ Helen thinks that people like their jobs if

a they get on well with their colleagues.
b there is a nice atmosphere at work.
c they are doing something they really enjoy.
d they get personal satisfaction from their work.

Unit 6: Problems and Advice

6a ◄ When you have a problem, who do you prefer to talk to about it?

a Watch video 6a. Match 1–4 with a–d to make sentences.

1 [d] When Mark has a problem, he prefers to discuss it with his
2 ☐ When Laurence has a problem, he prefers to discuss it with his
3 ☐ When Maibritt has a problem, she prefers to discuss it with her
4 ☐ When Colin has a problem, he prefers to discuss it with his

a husband, sister or friends.
b dad, girlfriend or mum.
c girlfriend or friends.
d best friend.

6b ◄ What advice would you give to a student who is worried about exams?

b Watch video 6b. Complete the sentences with the names in the box.

| Maibritt   Mark   Colin   ~~Laurence~~ |

1 __Laurence__ would tell the student not to get too worried about the exam.
2 _____ would tell the student not to panic because it's just an exam.
3 _____ would tell the student the exam isn't as important as it seems.
4 _____ would tell the student to relax and do their best.

6c ◄ What advice would you give to someone who can't sleep?

c Watch video 6c and tick (✓) the correct answers.

1 Maibritt thinks it's a good idea to read a _____ before you go to sleep.
   a ☐ magazine
   b ✓ book
   c ☐ newspaper

2 Colin thinks you should get plenty of exercise in the _____.
   a ☐ morning
   b ☐ afternoon
   c ☐ evening

3 Laurence thinks you shouldn't _____ before you go to sleep.
   a ☐ look at your phone
   b ☐ watch TV
   c ☐ play computer games

4 Mark thinks you should drink _____ before you go to sleep.
   a ☐ coffee
   b ☐ tea
   c ☐ milk

Vox pop video

Unit 7: Changes

7a ◄ Which life events do you think change most people?

a Watch video 7a. Match 1–3 with a–c to make sentences.
1. [c] Laurence thinks that people change when they
2. [ ] Darren thinks that people change when they
3. [ ] Peter thinks that people change when they

a get married or have children.
b do something new and exciting for the first time.
c go to university or start a new job.

7b ◄ How have you changed in the past five years?

b Watch video 7b. Complete the sentences with the names in the box.

| Peter   Laurence   Darren |

1 _____ thinks that now he is very careful about how he spends his time.
2 _____ thinks that he is more grown up now.
3 _____ thinks that has learnt a lot about himself.

7c ◄ Do you think people in this country are healthier now than they were twenty years ago?

c Watch video 7c and tick (✓) the correct answers.
1 Laurence thinks that when you go out …
 a [ ] it's hard to eat healthy food.
 b [ ] it's better to go to a fast-food restaurant.
 c [ ] it's easy to eat healthy food.
2 Peter thinks that most people …
 a [ ] are very fit and healthy.
 b [ ] are quite fit and healthy.
 c [ ] don't get much exercise.
3 Darren thinks that in general people …
 a [ ] smoke more than before.
 b [ ] smoke less than before.
 c [ ] are less healthy than before.

Unit 8: Culture

8a ◄ Is there a book you've liked since you read it at school?

a Watch video 8a and tick (✓) the correct answers.
1 Stephen _____.
 a [ ] reads more now than when he was at school
 b [✓] reads less now than when he was at school
 c [ ] has always read a lot of books
2 Malachi has read the Steinbeck novel _____ since he left school.
 a [ ] once
 b [ ] a few times
 c [ ] five times
3 Sammy _____.
 a [ ] enjoyed reading some of Shakespeare's plays
 b [ ] didn't enjoy reading Shakespeare's plays
 c [ ] can't remember any of the books he studied at school

8b ◄ Is there a sport or activity you've tried but didn't like?

b Watch video 8b. Match 1–4 with a–d to make sentences.
1 [c] Sammy
2 [ ] Stephen
3 [ ] Babs
4 [ ] Malachi

a wasn't very good at basketball because he was very short when he was young.
b has enjoyed all the sports she's tried.
c didn't like rugby because he was quite small when he was younger.
d enjoys doing all sports because he's very competitive.

8c ◄ Can you recommend a good film?

c Watch video 8c and tick (✓) the correct answers.
1 Sammy liked *Catch Me If You Can* because …
 a [ ] it was very exciting to watch.
 b [✓] the actors were very good.
 c [ ] it was very funny.
2 Stephen likes watching films because …
 a [ ] books take a long time to read.
 b [ ] they only last for two hours.
 c [ ] you can escape from your daily life.
3 Babs likes *Singing in the Rain* because of …
 a [ ] the acting.
 b [ ] the music.
 c [ ] the photography.
4 Malachi has watched *The Wolf of Wall Street* …
 a [ ] seven times.
 b [ ] four times.
 c [ ] three times.

Unit 9: Achievement

9a ◄ Is it important to go to university?

a Watch video 9a. Match 1–4 with a–d to make sentences.
1 [c] In Mark's opinion
2 [ ] In Carolyn's opinion
3 [ ] In Matt's opinion
4 [ ] In Lauren's opinion

a it isn't necessary to have a degree for some jobs.
b most companies prefer to employ people with degrees.
c it can be very useful to go to university if you want to have a specific career.
d it's important for young people to get the experience of living away from their parents.

79

9b ◀ What advice would you give to a student who doesn't like her university course?

b Watch video 9b and tick (✓) the correct answers.
1 Mark thinks that she should try and change it if _____ her course.
   a ✓ it's early in
   b ☐ it's late in
   c ☐ it's in the middle of
2 Carolyn thinks that perhaps she should change _____.
   a ☐ her university
   b ☐ her director of studies
   c ☐ one or two of her modules
3 Matt says that at a lot of universities students can change their _____ during the first year.
   a ☐ modules
   b ☐ course
   c ☐ tutor
4 Lauren thinks that she should _____.
   a ☐ talk to her friends
   b ☐ study something different
   c ☐ get a new job

9c ◀ What are the advantages of studying online?

c Watch video 9c. Complete the sentences with the names in the box.

| ~~Mark~~ Matt Lauren Carolyn |

1 In ____Mark____'s opinion you don't need to live near the university.
2 In _____'s opinion you can study when it suits you.
3 In _____'s opinion it's very good for people that have children.
4 In _____'s opinion you don't need to go to lectures that start early in the morning.

Unit 10: Values

10a ◀ What would you do if you found a bag of money in the street?

a Watch video 10a and tick (✓) the correct answers.
1 William says that he would _____.
   a ☐ keep it for himself
   b ☐ take it to the bank
   c ✓ take it to the police station
2 Mitchell says he would _____ if it was a small amount of money.
   a ☐ take it to the police
   b ☐ keep it for himself
   c ☐ spend it on new clothes
3 Shelby says that she would _____.
   a ☐ keep it for herself
   b ☐ take it to the police station
   c ☐ give it to her mum
4 Andy says that he would _____.
   a ☐ spend it on a nice holiday
   b ☐ keep it for himself
   c ☐ take it to the police station

10b ◀ How long would you queue in a shop before you gave up and left?

b Watch video 10b and tick (✓) the correct answers.
1 William would queue for …
   a ☐ five minutes.
   b ✓ ten minutes.
   c ☐ fifteen minutes.
2 Mitchell would usually queue for …
   a ☐ ten minutes.
   b ☐ twenty minutes.
   c ☐ thirty minutes.
3 Shelby would queue for …
   a ☐ ten minutes.
   b ☐ twenty minutes.
   c ☐ twenty-five minutes.
4 Andy would queue for …
   a ☐ five minutes.
   b ☐ ten minutes.
   c ☐ twenty minutes.
5 Adam would queue for …
   a ☐ 10–15 minutes.
   b ☐ 15–20 minutes.
   c ☐ 5–10 minutes.

10c ◀ Would you complain if you couldn't hear a film in the cinema because other people were too noisy?

c Watch video 10c and underline the correct words to complete the sentences.
1 William *doesn't mind* / <u>gets annoyed</u> / *doesn't do anything* if people are talking near him.
2 Mitchell *would complain* / *wouldn't complain* / *would change seats* if someone was talking near him.
3 Shelby would complain *immediately* / *after five minutes* / *after ten minutes* if someone was talking near her.
4 Andy would complain to *the people themselves* / *a cinema employee* / *the manager* if someone was talking near him.
5 Adam would complain to the *people that were making the noise* / *a cinema employee* / *the manager* if someone was talking near him.

Unit 11: Science & Discovery

11a ◀ Would you like to own any kind of robot?

a Watch video 11a. Complete the sentences with the names in the box.

| James   Dee Dee   Petros |

1 _____ would like to have a robot so that it could do the jobs around the house that she doesn't like doing.
2 _____ would like to have a robot so that he could have more time for working.
3 _____ would like to have a robot so that he could have more time for sleeping.

Vox pop video

11b◀ Have you started using any new technology recently?

b Watch video 11b. Match 1–4 with a–d to make sentences.
1 [c] Petros
2 [ ] Dee Dee
3 [ ] James
4 [ ] Ayden

a doesn't know much about information technology.
b owns a fully electric car.
c has had a smartphone for several years.
d likes to have the latest products.

11c◀ Can you think of three important inventions?

c Watch video 11c and tick (✓) the correct answers.
1 In Petros's opinion, the three most important inventions are …
   a [ ] the wheel, the car and computers.
   b [ ] the bicycle, the car and the telephone.
   c [✓] the wheel, the bicycle and the boat.
2 In Dee Dee's opinion, the three most important inventions are …
   a [ ] bicycles, cars and computers.
   b [ ] the Internet, computers and cars.
   c [ ] electricity, computers and the Internet.
3 In James's opinion, the three most important inventions are …
   a [ ] the wheel, the telephone and electricity.
   b [ ] the Internet, computers and the telephone.
   c [ ] cars, computers and the Internet.
4 In Ayden's opinion, the three most important inventions are …
   a [ ] the wheel, the bicycle and cars.
   b [ ] cars, boats and computers.
   c [ ] the bicycle, microwaves and the Internet.

Unit 12: Characters

12a◀ When you were a child, did you get on well with your brothers and sisters?

a Watch video 12a. Match 1–5 with a–e to make sentences.
1 [c] Lauren says that
2 [ ] Adam says that
3 [ ] Patrick says that
4 [ ] Oliviero says that
5 [ ] Dana says that

a she got on quite well with her sister when they were little.
b he always got on well with his brother and sister.
c she fought a lot with her brother when they were younger.
d he started getting on well with his older brother when he was about 15.
e he has the same interests as his younger brother.

12b◀ Can you remember something a teacher said to you when you were at school?

b Watch video 12b and tick (✓) the correct answers.
1 Lauren's teacher told her that if you make a mistake …
   a [ ] you'll get a bad mark.
   b [ ] it's too late to fix it.
   c [✓] you can start again.
2 When he was at school, Adam was …
   a [ ] hard-working.
   b [ ] naughty.
   c [ ] lazy.
3 Matteo's teacher said that …
   a [ ] he should believe in his own ability.
   b [ ] he wasn't very clever.
   c [ ] he should work harder.
4 Dana's teacher told her that it's important to …
   a [ ] study hard and play hard.
   b [ ] follow your dreams.
   c [ ] know your place in the world.

12c◀ What kind of things do you normally talk about with your friends?

c Watch video 12c and tick (✓) the correct answers.
1 Lauren and her friends usually talk about …
   a [ ] politics and sport.
   b [ ] fashion and the weather.
   c [✓] the news and fashion.
2 Adam and his friends usually talk about …
   a [ ] holidays, sport and fashion.
   b [ ] relationships, holidays and work.
   c [ ] the news, holidays and the meaning of life.
3 Patrick and his friends usually talk about …
   a [ ] cricket and football.
   b [ ] tennis and football.
   c [ ] basketball and tennis.
4 Matteo and his friends usually talk about …
   a [ ] sport, fashion and politics.
   b [ ] girls and life experiences.
   c [ ] work, the news and sport.
5 Dana and her friends usually talk about …
   a [ ] books, school and travel.
   b [ ] sport, fashion and politics.
   c [ ] work, books and holidays.

Audioscripts

Unit 1

1.1
1 birthday
2 bank
3 cinema
4 food
5 party
6 silly
7 music
8 sport
9 friendly
10 blog

1.2
ALICE What's Sarah doing in that shop?
NAOMI She's buying some postcards to send to her family.
A Really? I don't generally send postcards. I usually write a message on my Facebook wall. And sometimes I put a few photos of my holiday on my wall.
N Yes, me too, but Sarah's grandparents don't have a computer, so she sends them postcards instead.
A Oh, and what are Tom and Jack doing this morning?
N They're spending the day at the beach.
A But Tom doesn't like swimming in the sea. He says the water's too cold.
N Yes, but it's really hot today!

1.3
SAM Hi, James! Long time no see! How are you?
JAMES Hi, Sam. I'm fine, thanks. What a lovely surprise! Great to see you!
S Yes, it's really nice to see you, too.
J Where are you living these days?
S Oh, not far from here. In Park Road, near the sports centre.
J Oh, how nice!
S And this is my wife, Jackie.
J Your wife – wow! That's fantastic news! Nice to meet you, Jackie.
JACKIE Nice to meet you, too.

1.4
1 Sea View Road? Oh, how nice!
2 Your husband – wow! That's fantastic news!
3 We really must go. We're late.
4 What a lovely surprise!
5 Say hello to Roger for me.
6 Long time no see!
7 It was really nice to meet you.
8 We must meet up soon.
9 It was great to see you again.
10 When did we last see each other?

1.5
1 I'm pretty sure it was two months ago.
2 What a lovely surprise!
3 It was really nice to meet you.
4 I'm sorry, but I really must go.
5 Where are you living these days?
6 I'm late for a meeting.

1.6
PRESENTER When you move to a new school or town or start at university, it's important to make new friends. But it isn't easy. On today's programme new students at Princeton University tell us about how they are making friends during the first few weeks of term. First up is Richard.
RICHARD I don't particularly like going to parties and I hardly ever go to bars and discos so it was difficult for me to make friends. I like people who have something in common with so I joined the university walking club. We meet every Sunday and normally go for a walk into the forests or by the river near the university. It's good fun and I talk to lots of people.
PR Joining a club is a great way to meet new people. But there are other ways. Let's hear from Sophia, a nineteen-year-old student.
SOPHIA I'm studying Drama so I like talking to people. I'm not particularly interested in joining a club, as I generally prefer to meet people who like lots of different things. I posted a message on an online student network saying 'I'm looking for some friends. No rude or serious people. We can meet for a drink in the students' café every Tuesday.' About 10 people come each week. It's great fun and everyone is different.
PR But if you don't want to start your own group, there are other ways. Over to Peter.
PETER I don't really like using Facebook to make friends. I'm living in a large student house with about thirty other people so in the first week I knocked on everyone's bedroom door and said hello. Everyone here is friendly. Now I'm rarely on my own and there is often someone to talk to or go out with in the evenings.

Unit 2

2.1
depart   departed   look   looked
love   loved   post   posted
listen   listened   invite invited
hate   hated   enjoy   enjoyed
sound   sounded   like   liked

2.2
1 Were /wə/ you waiting for the bus?
2 I wasn't driving the car.
3 They were /wə/ watching TV.
4 We weren't having dinner.
5 She was /wəz/ talking on her phone.
6 Was /wəz/ she listening?
7 He wasn't smoking.
8 They weren't playing chess.

2.3
1 Is there anything else I can help you with?
2 Could you tell me where the information desk is?
3 How much is a return ticket to Edinburgh?
4 How often do the buses leave for the airport?
5 What time is the next coach to Barcelona?
6 Can I pay for my ticket in euros?
7 Where can I buy a sandwich for the journey?
8 How much does it cost to get a taxi to the airport?

2.4
A Excuse me.
B Yes, how can I help you?
A Could you tell me which platform the next train to London leaves from?
B Certainly, madam. It leaves from Platform 2.
A OK, thanks. And what time does it leave?
B It leaves at 10:32, in twelve minutes.
A Brilliant. Thanks.
B Is there anything else I can help you with?
A Actually, there is one more thing. Where can I buy a cup of coffee? Is there a café near here?
B Yes, there is. There's a café on the platform, over there.
A Great. Thanks so much.
B No problem. Have a good journey.

2.5
1 When did you check into your hotel?
2 How can I help you?
3 Did you get a visa when you went to China?
4 What time did you set off from home?
5 What time is your plane?
6 How much is a return ticket to Bath?

2.6
STEVE And now we go over to Susie with today's traffic and travel news. I hear it is particularly bad on the M3 and M4 motorways?
SUSIE Thanks, Steve, that's right. The heavy rain this morning caused problems on the M3. Four cars hit each other and because of that, there were long delays between London and Guildford. It doesn't look very good on the M4. A lorry broke down near Swindon about three hours ago and there was a huge traffic jam half an hour later. Peter from Bristol just texted on eight seven six six three two to say that there is a queue now. So if you need to get to Swindon this evening, you might want to go off the motorway and go on the main road – the A429. The M1 is looking a lot better today. There were no delays when I last checked, which is great for anyone who is going to the big music festival in Leeds tomorrow. However, the police have said that you must not hitchhike on the motorway. But if you haven't booked accommodation, you can take a tent and stay on a campsite in the park.
Unusually, there aren't many problems on the trains today, but if you are going away this weekend, lots of trains aren't working normally, so check before you go. If you are flying from Gatwick Airport, please phone your airline before you set off. The computer systems at the airport weren't working this morning and many flights were cancelled today. The computers are working now but there are long delays and even longer queues! Jackie and Bob phoned to say their flight to India was delayed by over twelve hours and they had to check into a hotel at the airport for the night. But I'm pleased to say that they've boarded their plane now and are on their way.
ST Well, I hope they've got a visa or they'll have another long queue when they arrive!
SU I hope so, too! It sounds like they're going to have a real adventure. Back to you, Steve.
ST Thanks, Susie. And here's the latest song by …

Unit 3

3.1
A Good morning. Can I help you?
B Er, yes. I'm looking for a present for my wife.
A Are you looking for anything in particular?
B Well, she loves earrings.
A Really? How about these earrings? They're really beautiful. A perfect present …
B Do you have anything cheaper?
A Well, these earrings here are cheaper. They're only £50 with the discount.
B Yes, I suppose she might like them. On second thoughts, maybe I should get something else.
A OK. Er, let me see … what about this necklace?
B Yes, it's lovely. OK, I'll take it.

3.2
1 Can you show us something else?
2 Can you enter your PIN, please?
3 I'm looking for a present for my husband.
4 Do you have any black jeans?
5 Thanks. I'll take it.
6 Actually, I think we should buy her a book.

3.3
DJ And now it's time for today's talking point. What's the nicest thing you have ever done for someone? Have you given something expensive away to someone or just made someone smile? Call, text or email me now. First on is Anita from Perth.
ANITA Hello, Baz. My neighbour hasn't got a job at the moment and it's her daughter's thirteenth birthday today. I know she couldn't afford to have a party so I thought I could help.
DJ And what have you done?
A I've borrowed a stereo from my brother and some disco lights from my friend. And we've turned part of her back garden into a beach with lots of sand I got at the local beach. Lots of the neighbours have given some food and we're going to have a beach party and disco this evening.
DJ That must have made your neighbour smile. Thanks for your call, Anita, and have a great night. What a nice woman. Next we have Gary from Adelaide. What's the nicest thing you've ever done?
GARY Hi, Baz. Last year I was in the city centre when a tourist asked me how to get to the museum. I gave him directions and then we started talking. He was from Greece and he was really friendly. Then it started raining really hard. He didn't have a coat so I lent him my umbrella. I asked him to bring it to my house when he was leaving Adelaide and then I forgot about it. Four days later he brought it to my house. I certainly didn't expect that. I invited him in and we had a cup of tea together. We got on well and we

82

Audioscripts

became friends. When he left, he invited me to visit him in Greece next summer. I've been saving up all year and I've just booked my ticket. I can't wait!

DJ That's a great story, Gary. Enjoy your holiday! Before we go, I've had an email from Mike in Darwin. He has started a group called 'Give someone a hug, make someone smile'. Every Sunday he walks around the city centre with his friends, giving people hugs and hopefully making them smile. Good luck with that, Mike – and be careful!

Unit 4

4.1
- **A** So what have you arranged for this evening?
- **B** Well, my parents are arriving at the station on the 6:30 train from Paris.
- **A** So, are you meeting them at the station?
- **B** Yes, we are. We're taking a taxi from our house at 6:00. I booked it this morning.
- **A** Good. So where are they staying?
- **B** At the Hilton Hotel. They've got a double room with a balcony.
- **A** Great. And what about the restaurant?
- **B** I've reserved a table for eight at eight o'clock. Everyone's coming to the restaurant at 7:45 so we can all be there when they arrive.
- **A** Brilliant. Have you told the restaurant that it's your father's birthday?
- **B** Yes, they've made him a special cake with HAPPY 60TH on it. They're bringing it to our table at ten o'clock, together with the coffee.
- **A** And what about tomorrow?
- **B** They aren't flying to Scotland until the afternoon, so there's plenty of time. Their flight's at 3:30.
- **A** Great, so it's all arranged. I have to go now because I'm meeting Sally for a coffee in ten minutes. See you later!

4.2
1. Are you going to go out tonight?
2. What are you going to do for your birthday?
3. He isn't going to have a holiday this year.
4. We're going to try to find a taxi.
5. I'm going to have a shower after breakfast.
6. They aren't going to do their homework.
7. She's going to phone her brother.
8. I'm not going to go to Ibiza this year.

4.3
1. We want to go swimming today.
2. They won't take you to the old castle.
3. I won't go to that restaurant again.
4. You want to wait for the next train.
5. I want to study English again next year.
6. Tom and I won't invite him to our party.

4.4
- **A** Are you doing anything on Wednesday? Would you like to go for a coffee?
- **B** Oh, that sounds nice. I'll just check. No, sorry, I can't do Wednesday. I'm going shopping with my mother.
- **A** Oh, OK, never mind. How about Friday? Is that OK for you?
- **B** Friday … hang on a minute … no, sorry. I'm going to London for the day. This week's really busy for me.
- **A** OK, so you can't do this week. What are you doing next Monday?
- **B** Next Monday? Just a moment, I'll just check. Nothing! I can do next Monday. Perfect!
- **A** Great! So we can meet for a coffee on Monday?
- **B** Yes, Monday's fine. Where shall we go?
- **A** Shall we meet at The Coffee Place at 11.00?
- **B** Brilliant! 11 o'clock. See you then.

4.5
1. Would you like me to bring anything?
2. Are you doing anything this Saturday?
3. This week's really busy for us.
4. What time shall we come round?
5. What are you doing on Tuesday next week?
6. Would you like to come round for lunch?
7. I can't do Thursday this week.
8. Is this Sunday OK for you?

4.6
1. I can't meet you tomorrow.
2. He can meet us at the station.
3. I didn't understand him.
4. She hasn't seen that film.
5. I must start cooking dinner.
6. They don't like basketball.

4.7
ISAAC What are your plans when you finish university this summer, Giles?
GILES Well, my brother Alex is getting married in July.
- **I** That's great news. Where is the wedding?
- **G** His fiancée Laura is Italian so it's going to be in her town in Tuscany in this magnificent old church there. The town is really pretty.
- **I** That sounds wonderful. Is it going to be a big wedding?
- **G** The party is in the town hall, which is huge. Laura's got a really big family.
- **I** Have you got to do anything at the wedding?
- **G** Yes, I have! I'm going to read a poem I wrote.
- **I** Brilliant! That's exciting. I guess you're going to need a new suit for that.
- **G** Yes, I've got to look my best, especially in front of all those Italian guests.
- **I** Really?
- **G** Yes, they always have great outfits. My dad's going to buy me a new suit if I pass my exams. Something really nice.
- **I** Great! Can you speak any Italian?
- **G** Si. Un po'! But I'm starting lessons next week. The Italian boy in our class, Gavino, is teaching me.
- **I** That's a good idea. How long are you going to Italy for?
- **G** I'm going for two weeks. I'm flying to Rome with my parents on the fourteenth of July and we're going to go sightseeing for a few days. My mum wants to see all the ancient buildings.
- **I** I love Rome. You can walk down a street of really cool modern buildings, then turn a corner and see something that's two thousand years old. It's amazing.
- **G** Wow, I can't wait to go.
- **I** Anyway, I've got to go. I'm going on a date tonight and I want to go to the hairdresser's before it closes.
- **G** OK, well make sure you have a shave before you meet her, Isaac.
- **I** Don't worry, I will. See you tomorrow then.
- **G** OK, see you.

Unit 5

5.1
1. Shall I lend you some money for the bus?
2. Maybe you should ask your manager for the day off.
3. I'll look up the train times on the Internet.
4. Do you want me to book a taxi for our guest?
5. Why don't I drive you to the airport?
6. How about arranging a meeting in Milan?
7. Why don't you borrow some money from your father?
8. You could catch a direct flight to Rome.

5.2
1. **A** Shall I book a room for your meeting?
   B Yes, good idea.
2. **A** Would you like me to drive you to the station?
   B No, I'll be fine. Don't worry about it. I can take the bus.
3. **A** But you won't be able to have any lunch.
   B Oh, never mind. I'm not really hungry.
4. **A** I'm really sorry. I can't come to the cinema tonight.
   B Oh, it doesn't matter. We can go another time.
5. How about asking your boss if you can have more time for the report?
6. Why don't I book the train tickets on the Internet?
7. Maybe you should invite your boss to the meeting, too?
8. You could send her some flowers for her birthday.

5.3
1. Would you like a coffee?
2. Yes, I would. Thanks.
3. Could you help me with my report?
4. Yes, of course I could.
5. You should get a taxi.
6. Yes, you're right. I should.
7. Shall I book a meeting room?
8. Well, what do you think? Shall I?

5.4
INTERVIEWER Thank you for coming, Josh. First of all, I'd like to talk about your CV. You have some good qualifications, but you've had a lot of different jobs in the last five years. Can you talk about those?
JOSH Yes, I worked as a postman when I finished university. I enjoyed working outside, but I had to work many hours each day and start early in the morning, which I hated, so I decided to look for other jobs.
- **I** So, you don't like working long hours then. Hmm. Tell me about your next job. You worked as a hairdresser, didn't you?
- **J** Yes, I did. I learned a lot of skills while I was there and I really liked the place. But I didn't like having to talk to people every day. I had to talk to the customers and make coffee.
- **I** Hmm. OK. What about your last job? You were an IT worker.
- **J** Yes, that was great. I earned a good salary and I worked with a nice team of people. Sometimes when we were busy I had to work at weekends, which wasn't great, but I usually just worked Monday to Friday. I didn't have to work with people so much, and I could often just sit at my desk and use the Internet, when we weren't busy, of course. And my manager didn't mind what time I started work.
- **I** And at what time did you usually start work?
- **J** The latest I could start was 10:30 am.
- **I** OK, Josh, so why would you like to work as a bank clerk for Mainland Bank?
- **J** I'd like to work in a team, and get some good experience of working in a bank. It looks like a nice environment to work in. And it also pays really well, too.
- **I** But you don't like working hard or dealing with people every day. Those are important parts of the job.
- **J** Well …
- **I** I'm sorry, Josh, but I don't think you're what we're looking for. Thanks for coming in today and good luck.
- **J** Oh. OK. I thought this would be a good job for me.
- **I** I don't think so. But good luck with your search. Goodbye.
- **J** Bye.

Unit 6

6.1
1. We took my grandmother to the theatre.
2. The children wanted to go to the zoo.
3. Where did you lose your mobile phone?
4. Would you like a cup of coffee?
5. Who did you invite to the party?
6. I don't think you should go to work today.
7. Could I borrow £5, please?
8. What did you think of the food?

6.2
1. **A** I think it's a good idea to book a table. The restaurant might be full.
   B Yes, I suppose so. Saturday night can be very busy.
2. **A** Someone stole my handbag when I was at the beach this afternoon.
   B How awful! I'm really sorry to hear that.
3. **A** I'd speak to your boss about it.
   B I don't think I should do that. She'll be angry with me.
4. **A** I wouldn't worry too much. You can get a new passport at the embassy.
   B Yes, you're right. I can go there one day next week.
5. **A** Do you think I should invite Steve to the surprise party?
   B No, I don't think that's a very good idea. Anna doesn't like him very much.
6. **A** What do you think I should do?
   B I think you should go to the police station.
7. **A** I didn't get the job in marketing.
   B Oh, what a pity. I'm sure you'll get another job soon.
8. **A** I broke my finger on Saturday.
   B Oh, that's a shame. So that means you can't play tennis today?

6.3
1. Which job do you think I should apply for?
2. I think you should ask your colleagues.
3. I'm really sorry to hear that.

83

4 Do you think I should look for a new job?
5 I think it's a good idea to speak to your boss.
6 I'd talk to your parents about it.
7 I wouldn't apply for the new marketing job.
8 I don't think you should leave your job.

▶ 6.4
1 You're from Canada, right?
2 Elena works in the Spanish Embassy.
3 Would you like to work in London?
4 We're having a surprise party for Anna.
5 My boss wants to speak to me.

▶ 6.5
MARSHA Hi, Georgia. How are you?
GEORGIA Hi. Not so good. I'm getting really annoyed with my little brother Jim at the moment. I'm trying to revise for my exams and he keeps stopping me from working. Sometimes he listens to his music very loudly late at night, sometimes he borrows something from me that I need to study, like my dictionary or laptop. I can't concentrate on my work for more than a few minutes. It's terrible.
MAR You should go and study in the library. It's really quiet there and you won't have to deal with the interruptions. I go there most weekends to study.
MAX You shouldn't have to go somewhere else. Ask your parents to deal with your brother. Your exams are more important than your brother. Your parents understand that.
G That's a good idea, Max. I'll ask my dad for help tonight. My brother will listen to him. And I'll also think about going to the library at the weekend. It's nice to have a change sometimes when you're studying. How's your revision going, Max?
MAX My problem is I just can't remember anything from History. I read a page and then ten minutes later I've forgotten it.
MAR That's not unusual. You should try writing down what you've just read. It's amazing how much more you will remember that way.
G And you should also record yourself speaking your notes and then you can listen to them on your MP3 player. You'll be surprised how much you can remember.
MAX Yes, I'll definitely try those ideas.
G Sometimes I even sing my notes. It's a bit embarrassing, but it will help you to remember lots of information.
MAX That's a brilliant idea.
MAR Any advice to help me understand Physics? It's so confusing. I look at it, I can read it, I can remember it, but when I think about it, I just don't understand it.
G It doesn't sound like Physics is your subject, Marsha. Perhaps you should do something else!
MAX That's not very nice, Georgia. I'm really interested in Physics. I'm happy to help you with it if you like, Marsha. I think you just need someone to explain it to you.
MAR Thanks, Max. I think that Georgia might be right, but I really want to pass the Physics exam this year, so I don't have to do it again next year. Are you free this weekend?
MAX No, I'm afraid not. I need to record all my history notes on to my MP3 player!

Unit 7
▶ 7.1
1 **A** So, what's the problem?
 B I've got a stomach ache. It's very painful.
2 **A** When did this start?
 B About two days ago.
3 **A** Where does it hurt? Can you show me?
 B Here, in this area.
4 **A** Can I have a look? So, does it hurt here?
 B Yes, it does. It hurts all the time. I can't get to sleep.
5 **A** Are you taking anything for the pain?
 B Yes, I've taken some aspirin.
6 **A** Well, I don't think it's anything to worry about.
 B Phew! That's good to hear.
7 **A** I think it's just indigestion.
 B Just indigestion? What a relief!
8 **A** I'll give you a prescription for some tablets. Take two every four hours.
 B Fine, thanks very much. Goodbye.

▶ 7.2
1 Don't worry. It's nothing to worry about.
2 Phew! That's good to hear.
3 It hurts all the time. I can't get to sleep.
4 Can I have a look?
5 Are you taking anything for the pain?
6 I feel sick and exhausted.
7 I think you'll need to see another doctor.
8 So, what's the problem?
9 What a relief!
10 You shouldn't stay in bed.

▶ 7.3
1 Do you do any exercise?
2 When did this problem start?
3 Could you take a few tests tomorrow?
4 How many aspirins have you taken?
5 How long have you had this problem?
6 Are you taking anything for the pain?
7 Do you have any allergies?
8 Have you had any accidents recently?

▶ 7.4
ORGANISER Welcome to the Lindfield School Reunion – a chance for students who finished school 20 years ago to meet again. It's great to see so many of our old classmates here and I hope that you will all have a brilliant evening. Drinks and dinner will be …
SEAN I haven't seen some of these people for at least 20 years. It's funny to see how everyone has changed.
SARAH I know. I was just talking to Stephen Downes. Do you remember him? He used to be really good looking. He was the most popular boy in our class.
SE Yes, I remember Stephen. Is that him over there?
SA Yes. He's put on a lot of weight, hasn't he? Apparently, he just got divorced from Jenny Robertson. She wanted him to go on a diet, and give up smoking and drinking coffee. But you know Stephen, he never liked doing what he was told.
SE Yes, I remember! So he hasn't changed that much then. Who's that attractive slim woman he's talking to? Isn't it Lisa Baker?
SA Yes, I was talking to her earlier. She used to be really overweight, didn't she? She was telling me that she went on a diet and started getting fit about 10 years ago. She's a lot more confident now and a lot healthier. She's just got engaged to a man from Germany.
SE I'm really pleased to hear that. I used to get on well with Lisa.
SA Have you seen Mike Andrews yet? You know, little Mike. He used to be really poor and always wore old clothes.
SE Yes, of course.
SA He arrived in a brand-new sports car. He started a computer company and got very rich. That's him talking to Laura Docherty, Emma Alexander and Rachel Edwards.
SE Wow! He looks great. And he seems to be a lot more popular than he used to be!
SA Ha, yes. Oh wow, look who's just arrived! It's Dale George. With Nicola Walker.
SE Yes, I saw they'd got together on Facebook. It's funny. They used to hate each other.
SA I know. They used to fight and argue all the time. They look really happy now.
SE Yeah. Oh, and what about Martin Dowd? Is he coming? I remember you used to really like him.
SA Yes, he was very popular. I got in touch with him last month to see if he was going to come. Unfortunately, he couldn't. He's getting married this weekend.
SE Again? Is that his third marriage?
SA Yes, that's right. Well, he used to have lots of girlfriends at school. I think he went out with five of the girls in our class.
SE Well, some people never change.
SA Yes, that's true.
O And now, ladies and gentlemen, please take your seats for dinner.

Unit 8
▶ 8.1
play squash   go surfing   do gymnastics
play golf   go snowboarding   do yoga
play volleyball go ice skating   do athletics
play tennis   go jogging   do judo
play football   go rock climbing   do aerobics
play ice hockey go skateboarding   do karate
play rugby   go scuba diving
                 go windsurfing

▶ 8.2
1 snowboarding   4 gymnastics
2 athletics   5 ice hockey
3 jogging

▶ 8.3
1 I meant to send you an email, …
2 I'm sorry I didn't come to your party.
3 I couldn't phone you last night …
4 I had to stay late at work yesterday.
5 Sorry, I didn't mean to make you worry.
6 I was going to call you, …
7 I'm sorry I didn't reply to your message, …
8 I had to visit my grandmother yesterday.

▶ 8.4
1 I meant to send you an email, but my computer wasn't working.
2 I'm sorry I didn't come to your party.
3 I couldn't phone you last night because my phone was dead.
4 I had to stay late at work yesterday.
5 Sorry, I didn't mean to make you worry.
6 I was going to call you, but I couldn't find your number.
7 I'm sorry I didn't reply to your message, but I've been so busy for the last two days.
8 I had to visit my grandmother yesterday.

▶ 8.5
MATT Now on Riverside Radio it's time for our weekly guide to what's on this weekend. As usual, we're going to talk to four listeners with very different interests about what they recommend doing this weekend. First of all, we'll talk to Rachel from Albany.
RACHEL Hi, Matt. There's lots happening this weekend if you like outdoor sports. Rock climbing at the Stirling Ranges has started again for the year. All of the climbing routes have been included in the new guidebook, which can only be bought at the information centre. But be careful! This is only for experienced climbers. But if water is more your thing, then the Margaret River Surfers will be out on the water somewhere in the area. Where they meet depends on the waves, but all the information you need is written on their website.
M Thanks, Rachel. That sounds like a lot of fun. Let's talk to Gareth now in Perth.
GARETH Hi, Matt. If you're interested in Italy and art, there's the Italian film festival. It includes films which have been directed by many of Italy's greatest directors and if you go to the art gallery, you can also see photographs of the actors in these films taken by the directors. The films will be shown at the Luna Palace Cinemas.
M Thanks a lot, Gareth. Let's talk to Virginia now in Fremantle. What's your weekend looking like?
VIRGINIA It's all about the written word in Fremantle this weekend. The annual poetry festival, which has been going for ten years, returns. As usual, the festival has been organised by the Fremantle Young Poets Society and includes something for everyone. The highlight this year must be the performance of 'bush poetry' by a group of young poets to music performed by local folk musicians *The Western Arc* on the beach at Wilson Park, south of Fremantle.
M A beach I've been to many times and a lovely place to hear some beautiful music and poetry. Finally, let's talk to Jenny in Bunbury. What's happening in Bunbury this weekend?
JENNY Well, it's time to get active in Bunbury this weekend. It's the annual 10 km race on Sunday. I've been training for the last three months for this, so I'm really looking forward to it. But if you

haven't done any training you're still welcome. Over 1,000 people will be running, jogging, or walking, and I'm sure everyone will enjoy the race, which was won last year by local athlete Jack Harding. It starts at 10 am.

M Well, good luck with it, Jenny. I hope you have a great time. I might come along to support you. So, it sounds like there are lots of things to do this weekend, for people who want to get active, and for those who prefer to get their brains working. I hope you've heard something that you're interested in doing and, most of all, I hope you have a great weekend.

Unit 9
▶ 9.1
1 I enjoy studying Maths at university, but I hate taking exams.
2 If you take notes in the lesson, it will be easier to revise for the exam.
3 I'm going to work harder next year so that I get better grades.
4 If she fails her exam, she'll have to take it again in January.
5 Although he got excellent grades, he didn't get a place at Oxford University.

▶ 9.2
A Is it possible to speak to Diane Smith, please?
B Certainly, I'll just put you through.
C Hello, Diane Smith's phone.
A Oh, hello. Is Diane there, please?
C No, I'm afraid she isn't available. She's in a meeting. Can I take a message?
A Yes, OK. Can you tell her that I called?
C Yes, of course. Who's calling, please?
A This is Paul Roberts speaking.
C OK. Shall I ask her to call you back?
A Yes, please. I'm here all morning.
C Has she got your number?
A Yes, she has.
C Fine. I'll ask her to call you back.
A Thanks. Bye.

▶ 9.3
PAM Oh, hello, is that Tom?
TOM Yes, it is.
P Hi, it's Pam here.
T Oh, hi, Pam.
P Is now a good time to talk?
T Well, I'm a bit busy.
P Sorry, Tom. I didn't catch that.
T Yes, I was just saying that I'm busy. Sorry, but I've got a meeting in five minutes. Can I call you back?
P Sure. Is everything OK?
T Yes, fine, but I've got to go.
P OK. Ring me when you're free.
T Speak to you soon. Bye.
P Bye.

▶ 9.4
1 The film starts at 8:50.
   The film starts at 8:15.
2 We're catching the nine o'clock bus.
   We're catching the ten o'clock bus.
3 My new boyfriend's name is James.
   My new boyfriend's name is John.
4 The programme is on BBC 1.
   The programme is on BBC 2.
5 We're going on holiday on Tuesday.
   We're going on holiday on Thursday.
6 I was born in 1990.
   I was born in 1991.

▶ 9.5
PROFESSOR Good morning, Gavino. Thanks for coming to see me this morning.
GAVINO Good morning, Professor.
P I'd like to talk to you about your work. There seem to be a few problems at the moment.
G Problems, Professor?
P Yes. The last two essays that you wrote for me were very poor. I really don't think that you had read any of the books. And you handed them both in late. I know that you're very busy at the moment, but so is everyone, and all the other students managed to do the essays on time.
G I'm sorry, Professor. I had six essays to write this term.
P I know that you only finished secondary school last year, but when you start a degree in Psychology, that's what you expect. If your next essay is late, I will refuse to mark it. OK?
G Yes, I understand.
P You've also avoided coming to my class for the last two weeks. If you don't come to class, you won't learn anything, Gavino. This is so important. Do you dislike listening to my lectures or have you got something better to do?
G No, of course not. I really regret not coming, but I was ill. But one of the other students agreed to lend me his notes.
P OK. Well, I recommend reading them very carefully. And if you don't understand something, come and talk to me. There are exams at the end of this term and if you don't attend every lecture, there is a good chance that you will fail.
G Yes, I know. I've started revising for them already.
P Well, that is good news. I've arranged to meet a group of students every Wednesday afternoon to talk about the exam. I think it would be very useful for you to join us.
G Yes, that sounds really useful. Unfortunately, I play rugby every Wednesday. My rugby is very important to me, Professor.
P And your degree isn't?
G Yes, that is very important too. Of course.
P Only 25 students every year get a place to study Psychology at this university. You are very lucky to be here. If your work doesn't get better, you may lose your place on the course. I want you to think very carefully about what is most important to you.
G I will, Professor.
P Have you got any questions that you want to ask me?
G Yes. There is something. Which books should I read?
P The books on the reading list.
G Which list is that?
P The list that I gave you at the start of the term.
G I don't think I have it.
P So you haven't read any of the books then.
G Er, no, I haven't.

Unit 10
▶ 10.1
1 If I had lots of money, I would buy an expensive sports car.
2 Would you marry him if he didn't live so far away?
3 If I were you, I wouldn't go swimming in the sea today.
4 If he asked her to go to Argentina with him, she probably would.
5 I would come and stay with you in New York if the flights weren't so expensive.
6 She wouldn't have to drive to work every day if she lived closer to her office.

▶ 10.2
1 decision
2 enjoyment
3 complaint
4 description
5 explanation
6 delivery
7 describe
8 complain

▶ 10.3
CUSTOMER Good morning. Could you help me, please?
SALES ASSISTANT Yes, of course. How can I help?
C I'd like to return this DVD, please.
SA Would you like to exchange it for something else?
C No, I'd just like a refund, please.
SA Do you have a receipt?
C No, I'm sorry, I don't. It was a present from my boyfriend, but I've already got it.
SA Well, I'm terribly sorry, but we don't give refunds without a receipt.
C Could I speak to the manager, please?
SA Yes, of course. I'll go and get him.
MANAGER What seems to be the problem?
C I'd like to make a complaint.

▶ 10.4
1 Excuse me, but this isn't what I ordered.
2 Is there anything wrong with it?
3 I'll ask someone to look at that for you right away.
4 We've been here for over an hour, but we still haven't ordered.
5 These shoes don't fit me because they're a bit small.
6 I'm terribly sorry, but we're extremely busy.
7 I've changed my mind and I've decided to keep it.
8 I'd like to exchange it for something else.
9 I'd like to return this watch, please.
10 What seems to be the matter?
11 I'll give you a full refund.
12 Your sales assistant hasn't been very helpful.

▶ 10.5
1 Can you check my bill, please?
2 Would you like me to give you a refund?
3 Did you bring your receipt with you?
4 Where did you buy it?
5 Could you wait a moment, please?
6 Can you take our order now, please?
7 Can I change these jeans for another pair?
8 Could you call the manager, please?

▶ 10.6
ZUZA Haluk, you buy a lot of things online, don't you?
HALUK Yes, I do. I think it's really convenient and usually much cheaper than going to a shop. You can go shopping when you feel like it and there are no queues to deal with. I'd do all my shopping online if I could.
Z And never leave your house! What I don't like is that you have to wait a few days for what you've bought to be delivered. That puts me off.
H That's true, but you don't have to wait too long, usually it arrives in one or two days.
Z What was the last thing you bought online?
H I bought a new coat last week.
Z I would never buy clothes online. You can't try them on.
H I saw a photo of the coat and there was also a good description of it.
Z And were you happy with it when it arrived?
H Not really. It was the wrong size. It was too small for me and the colour was different to the photo. The description wasn't very good either. The website said that it was a leather coat, but I don't think it is.
Z Did you complain?
H Yes, I wrote an email to the company and asked for a refund.
Z And what happened?
H They haven't replied yet.
Z Hmm. Well, if I were you, I'd phone them up and ask for a refund, and an explanation, too.
H Yes, I'll do that next week. I'm sure it will be fine.
Z I wouldn't carry on using that company though. Have you had any other problems buying things online?
H A few. Occasionally things break in the post. And sometimes the postman doesn't take care of something. I bought a book a few weeks ago and when it arrived it was completely wet. I think the postman had dropped it in some water. But it's usually fine. I buy lots of books and DVDs online. It's great, because you can find absolutely everything. There's so much more choice than at the local bookshop.
Z Yes, but I enjoy looking around the bookshop. It's really enjoyable.
H Me too. Sometimes I find the book in the shop and then buy it online! It's often a lot cheaper.
Z Hmm, but if everyone did that, there wouldn't be any more bookshops or music shops. That would be awful.
H I don't think that would happen.
Z It's happening at the moment. Lots of shops have closed down in our town because people shop online.
H Well, I'm going to carry on shopping online.
Z And I'm going to carry on going to the shops. It's fun, sociable and who knows, I might meet a handsome man in the poetry section of the bookshop. If you went shopping more, you might meet a nice girl. You certainly won't meet her sitting at home at a computer.

Unit 11
▶ 11.1
1 mountain climbing
2 computer screen
3 science fiction
4 address book
5 bread knife
6 car park
7 coffee cup
8 bookshelf

11.2

A Good morning. Please take a seat. I'll be with you in a moment … Now, how can I help you?
B Could you help us to find a hotel in London, please?
A Yes, of course. Would you like a hotel in the city centre?
B Yes, if possible.
A OK, how about the Hotel Stella? They've got some rooms free.
B Is it near an underground station?
A Yes, it is. It's about five minutes' walk from Marble Arch station. And it's very close to Hyde Park. It's one of the nicest hotels in London.
B Great. Can you ask if they have a double room for three nights? And can you check the price?
A Yes, sure. I'm afraid hotels in London are really expensive. A lot of people think that London's the most expensive city for tourists in the world.
B Yes, the hotel that we stayed in last year cost over £200 a night!
A Right, I've booked it for you. When you come out of the underground station, go along Edgware Road for about 200 metres and it's on the right, opposite a cinema.
B Brilliant. Thanks very much.

11.3

1 accidentally
2 on purpose
3 by chance
4 unfortunately
5 luckily
6 surprisingly
7 amazingly
8 fortunately
9 as expected

11.4

A Can you tell me where the Kensington Meeting Room is?
B Yes, sure. It's on the first floor. Go through that door over there. Then go down to the end of the corridor. Then go up the stairs to the first floor. At the top of the stairs, turn left along another corridor. The Kensington Room is the fourth door on the right.
A Great, thanks.

11.5

1 Go down the stairs to the ground floor.
2 Go through those doors and then down the corridor.
3 So first go along the corridor to the stairs?
4 Could you tell me where the staff restaurant is, please?
5 Then go down the corridor and it's the first office on the right.
6 Go up the stairs to the third floor.
7 So, can I just check?
8 Right, I think I've got that.
9 At the top of the stairs, turn right and go along another corridor.
10 The meeting room is the second door on the left.

11.6

1 bored
2 fur
3 sir
4 short
5 ward
6 earl
7 Paul
8 worm

11.7

REPORTER Police are looking for two men who stole money from a cash machine outside Western Bank in Harris Road, Bakersfield at midnight last night. The men arrived at the bank in a large car and crashed into the cash machine on purpose four times. Margaret Edwards is the woman who saw what happened.

MARGARET I live opposite the bank and was in bed at the back of the apartment. But just before midnight, I got up to go to the bathroom. When I heard a car going very fast, I went into the front living room and looked out the window. I've never seen anything like it. The car drove up to the cash machine at about 50 miles per hour and didn't stop. I thought it was an accident, but amazingly they did it again and again. I called the police immediately.
R What did the men do next?
M They got out of the car, put on some gloves and tried to break the cash machine open with a baseball bat which they got from the back of the car. Fortunately, they couldn't open the machine but then, the driver got back into the car and drove into it again.
R Can you describe the men?
M Yes, I can. Fortunately, there were street lights on, so it was easy to see them. The man who was driving the car was about 20 years old, very tall and with very short hair. The other man was about the same age, was short and had dark hair, a hat and sunglasses.
R Erm … how long did it take them to get the machine open?
M Unfortunately, the second time the machine broke and they could steal some money. Luckily, the police also arrived at this time so the men only managed to take a small amount of money. They quickly jumped back into the car and tried to drive off. But they drove backwards into a road sign and then, unsurprisingly, the car didn't start because it was so damaged. So they got out and ran away down Park Avenue.
R Did the police go after them?
M Yes, the police car followed them, but the men ran into the park and disappeared.
R I hear that you found something nearby.
M Yes, I found a key ring with the name Terry on it and a house key. It was next to the car. I think one of the men dropped it. I gave it to the police when they came back.
R And what about the car?
M The police think that the men stole it from a car park earlier in the day.
R Thank you, Mrs Edwards. Photos of the two men which were taken by security cameras outside the bank will be on the TV programme *Everyday Criminals* on RBC1 tonight at 8. And now, over to Adam with today's sports news.

Unit 12

12.1

brought
come
done
fallen
known
spoken
run
taught
woken
won

12.2

1 careless
2 serious
3 selfish
4 easy going
5 reliable
6 confident
7 patient
8 anxious
9 generous
10 creative

12.3

1 A I believe yoga is a great way to relax before you go to bed.
 B You're absolutely right. I try and do a few exercises every night.
2 A I think Brazil have the best football team in the world.
 B I'm not sure about that. I think Argentina will beat them in the final.
3 A In my opinion, Venice is a more attractive city than Florence.
 B Definitely. It's such a beautiful place to visit. I love it!
4 A This is a nicer cinema than the one we went to last week.
 B I agree. The seats are very comfortable and the screen is wider.
5 A Barcelona is the biggest city in Spain.
 B I don't think so. I think there are more people in Madrid, actually.
6 A Leonardo DiCaprio is a better actor than Brad Pitt.
 B That's true. He was brilliant in *The Great Gatsby*.
7 A In my view, Italian coffee is better than French coffee.
 B I'm sorry, but how do you know? You don't drink coffee!
8 A I think the weather in the UK in winter is much better than in Germany.
 B I'm afraid I don't agree. Here it rains so much in January and February. I can't stand it!

12.4

1 A I think the Amazon is the longest river in the world.
 B I don't think so. Actually, I think the Nile is longer than the Amazon.
2 A Swiss chocolate is much nicer than British chocolate.
 B You're absolutely right. It's probably the best in the world.
3 A Russian is a harder language to learn than Spanish.
 B Definitely. In my view, Spanish is one of the easiest languages to learn.
4 A Everybody should retire when they reach sixty.
 B Oh, please. That's much too early! Older people have so much experience which they can pass on to their younger colleagues.
5 A Tablets are so much more practical than laptops.
 B That's true. They're much lighter and easier to carry.
6 A His last film was brilliant!
 B You're right. It's the best film he's made so far.

12.5

1 A Antonio Banderas is a Mexican actor.
 B Er, he's actually a Spanish actor.
2 A French food's the best in the world.
 B Well, actually, I think Italian food is the best.
3 A I like the American English accent.
 B Do you? I prefer British English, actually.
4 A New York's the best place to live in the USA.
 B Actually, I think San Francisco's the best place.
5 A I think Chelsea will win the Champions League this year.
 B No way! Barcelona will win it this year.
6 A Baseball is the most popular sport in the USA.
 B I'm sorry, but I think American football is the most popular sport.

12.6

DAISY So, where have you been in India so far, Brad?
BRAD I flew into Delhi and took the train down across to Jaipur. I'm going to Goa next. Have you been there, Lewis?
LEWIS Yeah, Goa's cool. We're going to Kerala. How's your trip been so far, Brad?
B Apart from the mosquitoes and the spiders, pretty good. I had a great time in Delhi. I stayed with this Indian guy, Raj, who I'd met through the website Couchsurfing.org. He was really sociable and took me to some really amazing places.
D Yeah, we've met some great Indian people. Really friendly and generous.
B Yeah, but not everyone. I had a pretty bad time in Jaipur.
D What happened?
B I met these two brothers, Jay and Vikram, in a tea house. Jay was really funny and confident. He knew a lot about California. Viki was older and a bit more sensible. They offered to show me around and they seemed reliable so I agreed. We went sightseeing and they told me about their lives. Viki said that they could take me to see some tigers the next day if I wanted.
L Sounds cool.
B Well, then they started telling me about their business. They sold jewellery. They took me to their factory and showed me around. Then they tried to sell me some. I didn't want to, but in the end I said I would buy a small piece. They said it would be ready the next day and then took me back to my hostel. The next day I felt a bit anxious, but went to their factory to collect the jewellery. They had made my piece and had made 30 other necklaces too. They said that this was what I had asked for the day before. They told me that I would have to pay 100 dollars for the jewellery. I had only taken 10 dollars with me when I left that morning. Jay said that he would take me to a cash machine to get the money. I hadn't taken my credit card with me, but I didn't tell him that. We drove to a bank and we all got out. I didn't know where I was, but I decided to run away. I started running and Jay followed me. But I was faster and after a few minutes I was safe. I waited behind a dustbin in a small street for a while and then went onto the main road and found a taxi. The driver could see how anxious I was and drove me back to the hostel. I told him what had happened and he was quite angry with them. He was really generous and didn't charge me anything. The next day I took the first train out of Jaipur!
L Sounds awful. But hey, that's a pretty cool story you've got.
D Yeah.
B Yeah, I know. I'm sure you've got some stories. And we've got another three hours on this train!
L No worries, mate. So, we were in Varanasi …

Answer key

Unit 1

1A

1

a 2 serious 3 delicious 4 gorgeous 5 silly 6 lovely

b 2 delicious 3 perfect 4 strange 5 **B** alright 6 awful 7 amazing 8 rude

2

a 2 did you meet 3 Did he grow up 4 was the film like 5 did you pay 6 Why did she go 7 did he make 8 was your holiday

b 2 Does he work in a bank?
3 Why did you go to New York last month?
4 What is that new Brazilian restaurant like?
5 Who was that man with your sister?
6 What type of TV programmes do you watch?
7 Which university did you go to?
8 How much did the tickets cost?

1B

1

a 2 I particularly enjoy watching old Hollywood movies.
3 She absolutely hates it when people are late for meetings.
4 We generally go to Italian restaurants, but sometimes we also go to Turkish ones.
5 We're pretty sure his flight arrives at Terminal 2, but I need to check it.
6 I really hope she brings her gorgeous brother to the party!

b 2 hardly ever 3 normally 4 fairly 5 really 6 rarely 7 mainly 8 pretty

2

a long vowel: 3, 4, 5, 7, 8

3

a 2 go 3 'm reading 4 wants 5 are you waiting 6 visit 7 's studying 8 're playing

b 2 's buying 3 don't 4 send 5 write 6 put 7 don't have 8 sends 9 are Tom and Jack doing 10 're spending 11 doesn't like 12 's

1C

1

a 2 What a 3 to see you 4 these days 5 far from 6 how 7 this is 8 news 9 meet 10 too

c 2 news 3 must 4 surprise 5 hello 6 time 7 meet 8 up 9 again 10 last

2

a 2 lovely, surprise 3 really, nice, meet 4 sorry, must, go 5 Where, living 6 late, meeting

1D

1

a c

b True: 2, 5; False: 1, 3, 4, 6

2

a 2 Yesterday we visited the Palace of Versailles near Paris.
3 In the mornings, I usually go to the beach with my Portuguese friends.
4 I hope you're having a lovely time in Canada with your family.
5 Their English is very good, but we always speak in German.

3

a **Suggested answer:**
Hi Paul
Hope you're having a good holiday in Ireland.
I'm spending two weeks with my brother and his family here in Turkey. I don't speak Turkish, but my brother's wife and his three children speak very good English, so communication isn't a problem.
They live about 30 km from Istanbul in a small town on the Bosphorus. It's very hot at the moment, but they have a lovely swimming pool near their house, so we go swimming there every day.
I'm visiting lots of amazing places with my brother's family. Yesterday we went to the Grand Bazaar in the centre of Istanbul. It's an enormous indoor market and there are over 3,000 shops. I'm sending you a photo of it. I bought a lovely leather handbag.
My brother's house has a big garden, so we usually have dinner outside in the evenings, when it isn't so hot. We normally eat at about ten o'clock. My sister-in-law's a brilliant cook, so the food is delicious!
I'm having a lovely time in Turkey.
See you back at work next month.
Becky

Reading and listening extension

1

a 2 c 3 a

b 2 b 3 c 4 c 5 a 6 b

2

a 2 a 3 b

b 2 a 3 b 4 c 5 a 6 b

Review and extension

1

2 At the moment, she's working in the café by the station. / At the moment, she is working in the café by the station.
3 Why did you miss the bus?
4 I can't talk to you now because I'm doing my homework.
5 What kind of music do you usually listen to?
6 They're waiting for the bus to London. / They are waiting for the bus to London.

2

2 We really enjoyed the film last night.
3 We had a lovely time at the party last night.
4 I think our History lessons are so boring.
5 I think that man's a bit strange. Look, he's talking to himself.
6 New York's all right, but I prefer living in London, actually. / New York's alright, but I prefer living in London, actually.

3

2 h 3 a 4 c 5 g 6 f 7 b 8 d

Unit 2

2A

1

a 2 I slept very badly on the plane, so I felt very tired the next day.
3 Did you take the train from New York to Washington?
4 Correct
5 They spent two nights in a hotel and then they stayed at a friend's house for three days.
6 I didn't enjoy my trip to Scotland because the weather wasn't very good.
7 Correct
8 Correct

b 1 **B** didn't sleep, weren't 2 **A** did you do **B** didn't have, decided
3 **A** did Ben go **B** went 4 **A** Did you bring **B** did, bought
5 **A** Did you meet **B** did, met 6 **A** Did you visit **B** didn't have

2

a 2 e 3 a 4 f 5 h 6 b 7 c 8 g

b 2 passport 3 backpack 4 guidebook 5 foreign currency 6 suitcase

3

a hated, sounded, posted, invited

87

2B

1

a 2 hitchhiked 3 gave 4 set off 5 missed 6 took off 7 landed
8 boarded 9 changed 10 got to

b 1 **B** crash 2 **A** miss **B** got lost 3 **A** long delays **B** strike
4 something wrong 5 queue, broke down 6 **B** turbulence

2

a 2 was snowing 3 Were you flying 4 were you driving 5 were you standing
6 wasn't working

b 2 was driving 3 broke down 4 missed 5 bought 6 were waiting
7 started 8 decided 9 took 10 bought

3

a 1: c, e, f; 2: b, g; 3: d, h

2C

1

a 2 Could you tell me where the information desk is?
3 How much is a return ticket to Edinburgh?
4 How often do the buses leave for the airport?
5 What time is the next coach to Barcelona?
6 Can I pay for my ticket in euros?
7 Where can I buy a sandwich for the journey?
8 How much does it cost to get a taxi to the airport?

c 2 can 3 Could you 4 from 5 what time 6 anything else 7 Actually
8 near here 9 over there 10 Have

e 2 b 3 f 4 d 5 h 6 g 7 e 8 a

2

a 2 a 3 a 4 b 5 a 6 a

2D

1

a 1 d 2 c

b True: 2, 3, 5; False: 1, 4, 6

2

a 2 because 3 but 4 and 5 because 6 When 7 so 8 but

3

a Suggested answer:
Carlos and I got to New York at 14:30 this afternoon. It was a very long flight from Madrid and we were very tired when we arrived because we couldn't sleep on the plane. When we got off the plane the first thing we noticed was the cold – minus six degrees! It was freezing! Everything they say about New York is true! The people at the airport weren't very friendly and we couldn't understand them because they spoke so quickly. In the end we took the subway from JFK Airport to the city centre. We're staying at The Crowne Plaza Hotel near Central Park. The hotel is full of European tourists and everyone was very friendly and helpful. Carlos is telling me to get ready to go and eat, so I have to finish now – more tomorrow.

Reading and listening extension

1

a 2 a, c 3 a, d

b 2 Carl and Sam 3 Carl and Sam 4 Ashish and Bryony
5 Ashish and Bryony

c 2 sunny 3 lift 4 cost 5 morning

2

a 2 e 3 c 4 d 5 b

b 2 c 3 a 4 b 5 b 6 a

Review and extension

1

2 When we got to the station, the train was just arriving.
3 My wife phoned me while I was waiting for my plane.
4 A man took my wallet while I was waiting in the queue for my ticket.
5 Last year, we went on holiday to Greece for two weeks.
6 I was driving to the airport when I saw the accident.

2

2 My journey from Berlin to London took fifteen hours.
3 Last week, I went to Rome on a business trip.
4 The traffic was terrible because it was the rush hour.
5 By the time they checked out of the hotel, it was 2 pm.
6 In the afternoon, they went sightseeing in the old town.

3

2 set 3 took 4 fell 5 75% 6 drove 7 I'm 8 are

Unit 3

3A

1

a 2 Have you ever been to the carnival in Rio de Janeiro?
3 I have given money to charity twice this week.
4 You have never helped me with my homework.
5 Have they ever done any volunteer work?
6 She has never left a big tip for the waiter.
7 Have you ever given any money to a homeless person?
8 I have visited my grandmother several times this month.

b 1 **B** gave
2 **A** Has she ever done **B** did
3 **A** Have you ever helped **B** helped
4 **A** 've left / have left **B** did you leave
5 **A** Has he ever bought **B** bought

2

a 2 h 3 e 4 b 5 g 6 c 7 f 8 a

b 2 give 3 did 4 gave 5 do 6 made 7 doing 8 given

3B

1

a 2 g 3 a 4 h 5 e 6 c 7 d 8 b

b 2 into 3 bank account 4 afford 5 lend 6 borrow 7 spend 8 loan
9 back

2

a 2 yet 3 just 4 already 5 **B** just 6 already 7 just 8 yet

b 2 He's already borrowed £2,000 from his bank. / He has already borrowed £2,000 from his bank.
3 Have you paid Louise back yet?
4 Sue has already spent the money she borrowed from me. / Sue's already spent the money she borrowed from me.
5 We've just bought a new TV in the sales. / We have just bought a new TV in the sales.
6 Has she saved enough money to buy a tablet yet?
7 I've already bought a present for my wife. / I have already bought a present for my wife.
8 They've just opened a new bank account in France. / They have just opened a new bank account in France.

3C

1

a 8, 1, 6, 9, 10, 3, 2, 5, 4, 7

c 2 for 3 in 4 next 5 On second thoughts 6 enter 7 size
8 something else

d 2 I think I'm a size 14.
3 Do you have the same one in blue?
4 Can you tell me how much it is?
5 That's a bit too expensive.
6 Do you have a cheaper one?

2

a 2 enter, PIN 3 present, husband 4 black, jeans 5 Thanks, take
6 Actually, book

3D

1

a c

b True: 2, 3; False: 1, 4

Answer key

2
a 7, 5, 2, 4, 1, 3, 6

3
a Suggested answer:
Hello everyone
This email is to say a big 'Thank you!' to everyone who helped us to raise money for Save the Children over the past twelve months. We have successfully raised £495!
Most of you came to the Save the Children sports day in September. That was a brilliant event and we all had lots of fun. A lot of you also came to our 1990s karaoke evening in October. And, of course, next week there's our popular quiz night with big prizes for the winning team.
Save the Children will use our money to save children's lives and to give them a future. Last year, Save the Children helped ten million children around the world. A small amount can make a big difference. For example, just £3 can save the lives of eight children with stomach virus.
Would you like to help us raise more money for Save the Children? Email us and we can tell you about our future events. Thanks again for all your help.

Reading and listening extension

1
a 2 100   3 13 million   4 10 million
b True: 1, 3, 5; False: 2, 4
c 2 wrote   3 cost   4 called   5 spend   6 get   7 borrow   8 save   9 bought

2
a 2 Anita   3 Mike   4 Anita   5 Gary
b 2 b   3 a   4 b   5 c   6 b

Review and extension

1
2 Have you ever given money to charity?
3 I went to China on business last year.
4 I've just bought a new mobile phone. / I have just bought a new mobile phone.
5 I haven't bought a birthday present for my brother yet.
6 I've already spent £200 this weekend. / I have already spent £200 this weekend.

2
2 Can you lend me 50 euros, please?
3 Joe made a really funny joke, but nobody laughed.
4 James is saving up for a new computer.
5 Our taxi driver was very friendly, so we gave him a big tip.
6 I bought a new laptop in the sales – it was only £150!
7 Have you ever done any volunteer work?
8 Tony owes me £50, but he hasn't paid it back yet.

3
2 in time   3 under   4 like   5 about   6 over   7 spoken   8 a beginner

Unit 4

4A

1
a 2 tie   3 jumper   4 sweatshirt   5 earrings   6 tights   7 tracksuit   8 underwear   9 sandals   10 high heels   11 bracelet   12 flat shoes

2
a 2 Are you going to invite your cousin to your wedding?
3 They aren't going to get married this year.
4 What are you going to do after university?
5 We're going to visit my relatives in Spain next year.
6 What are you going to wear to the party?
b 2 are   3 meeting   4 're taking   5 are   6 staying   7 's coming   8 're bringing   9 aren't flying   10 'm meeting

3
a 2 gonna   3 going to   4 going to   5 gonna   6 gonna   7 going to   8 going to

4B

1
a 2 h   3 g   4 b   5 f   6 a   7 d   8 e
b 1 **B** 'll   2 **B** 'll   3 shall   4 won't   5 **A** Shall **B** 'll   6 won't   7 Shall   8 **B** 'll

2
a Across: 5 indoor   7 high   8 ordinary   10 peaceful; Down: 1 modern   2 narrow   3 magnificent   6 noisy   9 huge
b 2 pretty   3 outdoor   4 quiet   5 modern   6 high

3
a 2 won't   3 won't   4 want to   5 want to   6 won't

4C

1
a 3, 10, 5, 2, 1, 6, 7, 4, 9, 8
c 2 Are you doing anything this Saturday?
3 This week's really busy for us.
4 What time shall we come round?
5 What are you doing on Tuesday next week?
6 Would you like to come round for lunch?
7 I can't do Thursday this week.
8 Is this Sunday OK for you?
e 2 Mum   3 to the cinema   4 work conference   5 in Blackpool   6 Saturday

2
a 2 meet, <u>station</u>   3 didn't, under<u>stand</u>   4 <u>has</u>n't, seen, film   5 must, start, <u>dinner</u>   6 don't, like, <u>bas</u>ketball

4D

1
a d
b True: 2, 4; False: 1, 3, 5

2
a 2 Thanks for inviting me to your party.
3 It would be lovely to see you.
4 We're free on Saturday and we'd love to come.
5 This is just to say that we're having a party on Saturday.
6 We haven't seen you for ages!

3
a Suggested answer if she can go:
Hi Sam
Lovely to hear from you. Yes, I'm fine, thanks. My new job is brilliant, but I'm working very hard.
Thanks for inviting me to your birthday party. I'm free next Saturday and I'd love to come. Don't worry. I'll bring a huge salad! I'm looking forward to seeing you and having a nice chat.
All the best
Jess

Suggested answer if she can't go:
Hi Sam
Nice to hear from you. Yes, I'm fine, thanks. My new job is brilliant, but I'm working very hard.
Thanks for inviting me to your birthday party on Saturday. I'm really sorry, the party sounds like fun but I'm afraid I can't come. I'd love to come, but I'm visiting my cousin in Paris next weekend.
Hope you have a nice birthday party. See you soon anyway.
Love
Jess

Reading and listening extension

1
a 6, 4, 5, 3, 2, 1
b True: 2, 3, 5; False: 1, 4
c 2 going to have, hasn't bought / has not bought
3 is going to / 's going to
4 is getting ready / 's getting ready
5 is arriving / 's arriving

2
a 2 Alex   3 Gavino   4 Alex's mum   5 Isaac
b 2 b   3 b   4 c   5 b

Review and extension

1
2 Don't worry. I will pay the money back tomorrow. / Don't worry. I'll pay the money back tomorrow.
3 He's going to buy a new car next month. / He is going to buy a new car next month.
4 Shall I come to your house in half an hour?
5 Shall we go to that café for a cup of tea?
6 Are you going to do your homework this evening?

2
2 Are you going to buy a new suitcase in the sales?
3 I love it here in the country. It's so peaceful!
4 He always wears a tie when he goes for a job interview.
5 I love coming to this park because you can't hear the traffic. It's so quiet here.
6 That restaurant's so noisy. It's really hard to talk there.

3
2 for 3 forward 4 after 5 around 6 up

Unit 5

5A

1
a 2 hairdresser 3 plumber 4 scientist 5 banker 6 electrician 7 lawyer 8 accountant 9 dentist 10 nurse

b 2 salary 3 training 4 environment 5 team 6 university degree 7 people 8 self-employed 9 skills 10 qualifications

2
a 2 can't 3 can't 4 have to 5 have to 6 can't

b 2 can't 3 don't have to 4 have to 5 doesn't have to 6 has to 7 has to 8 mustn't 9 has to 10 doesn't have to

5B

1
a 2 h 3 a 4 g 5 b 6 f 7 e 8 d

b 2 might 3 won't 4 might not 5 will / 'll 6 A will / 'll B will 7 might 8 won't

2
a 2 carer 3 computer programmer 4 vet 5 designer 6 architect 7 musician 8 actor 9 journalist 10 postman 11 shop assistant 12 politician

b 2 builder 3 musician 4 architect 5 shop assistant 6 actor 7 carer 8 computer programmer 9 journalist 10 designer 11 postman 12 politicians

5C

1
a 2 Maybe you should ask your manager for the day off.
3 I'll look up the train times on the Internet.
4 Do you want me to book a taxi for our guest?
5 Why don't I drive you to the airport?
6 How about arranging a meeting in Milan?
7 Why don't you borrow some money from your father?
8 You could catch a direct flight to Rome.

c 1 B idea 2 A Would B fine, worry 3 B mind 4 A sorry B matter 5 about 6 don't 7 Maybe 8 could

2
a 2 strong vowel 3 weak vowel 4 strong vowel 5 weak vowel 6 strong vowel 7 weak vowel 8 strong vowel

5D

1
a c

b True: 1, 3, 4, 6; False: 2, 5

2
a 2 f 3 d 4 a 5 h 6 c 7 b 8 e

3
a **Suggested answer:**
Dear Sir/Madam,
I am writing to apply for the job of sales assistant, which you advertised in The Argus newspaper.
I am a student at the University of Sussex and I am available to work from October.
A job with you will be an exciting opportunity for me to learn new skills and to work in a new environment. I have a lot of experience of working in sales. Last summer I worked for three months in a very busy shop selling mobile phones and tablets and I think this experience will be very useful in this job.
I attach a copy of my CV with more details about my previous employment.
Could you give me more information about the salary and working hours, and also more details of your training programme?
I look forward to hearing from you.
Yours faithfully,

Reading and listening extension

1
a 1 a 2 c 3 d 4 b

b 2 is doing something they love
3 gets paid well, is doing something they love, (sometimes) has to work many hours every day
4 gets paid well, works and studies, is doing something they love, has to work many hours every day

c 2 b 3 a 4 c 5 a, d

2
a 2 Postman, Hairdresser, Bank clerk 3 Hairdresser 4 IT worker, Bank clerk 5 IT worker, Bank clerk

b 1 early
2 skills, people/customers/clients
3 starting, weekends

Review and extension

1
2 Excuse me, sir. You mustn't smoke on the plane. It's against the law. / Excuse me, sir. You must not smoke on the plane. It's against the law.
3 Do you have to wear a suit to work?
4 When I finish school, I might go to university. It depends on my grades. / When I finish school, I may go to university. It depends on my grades.
5 I have to start work at 7 o'clock in the morning in my new job!
6 I'll take my umbrella. It might rain this afternoon. / I'll take my umbrella. It may rain this afternoon.

2
2 My sister works as a shop assistant in a big department store.
3 You need good qualifications if you want to become a doctor.
4 He works as a designer for a top fashion magazine.
5 If you want to become a plumber, you'll need to go to college.
6 My brother wants to become a professional musician.

3
2 job 3 work 4 work 5 work 6 work 7 work 8 jobs 9 work

Unit 6

6A

1
a 2 go 3 Don't sit 4 shouldn't have 5 Eat 6 shouldn't drink 7 don't use 8 should read 9 should have 10 should go

b 2 Eat lots of fruit and vegetables every day. / You should eat lots of fruit and vegetables every day.
3 Don't use your computer for very long in the evenings. / You shouldn't use your computer for very long in the evenings.
4 You should try to relax for an hour before you go to bed. / Try to relax for an hour before you go to bed.
5 I think she should get more exercise during the day.
6 You shouldn't go swimming immediately after lunch.
7 When you've got a headache, take an aspirin. / When you've got a headache, you should take an aspirin.
8 Don't stay at work after 6 o'clock.

2
a 2 h 3 d 4 g 5 f 6 a 7 b 8 c

b 2 on 3 for 4 about 5 for 6 on 7 from 8 for

Answer key

3
a 2 long 3 long 4 short 5 long 6 short 7 short 8 long

6B
1
a 2 exciting 3 interested 4 shocked 5 annoyed 6 tiring 7 amazing 8 embarrassed

b 2 confused 3 interesting 4 surprising 5 frightened 6 disappointed 7 shocking 8 excited

2
a
2 It was interesting to learn about sharks.
3 Can you tell us where to park our cars?
4 It is dangerous not to wear a seat belt.
5 She had a bath to help her relax.
6 They went to the station to meet their aunt.
7 She phoned her father to ask him for some money.
8 He didn't know what to wear to the party.

b
2 He asked me how to get to the airport.
3 She was annoyed not to receive an invitation to his wedding.
4 They went to the supermarket to buy some food for dinner.
5 We couldn't remember which bus to catch for the airport.
6 John and Angela decided not to have their wedding in Scotland.
7 It was embarrassing to fail my driving test again.
8 She went to the library to borrow a book on dinosaurs for her son.

6C
1
a 2 e 3 f 4 g 5 c 6 h 7 a 8 b

c
2 I think you should ask your colleagues.
3 I'm really sorry to hear that.
4 Do you think I should look for a new job?
5 I think it's a good idea to speak to your boss.
6 I'd talk to your parents about it. / I'd talk about it to your parents.
7 I wouldn't apply for the new marketing job.
8 I don't think you should leave your job.

2
a 2 a 3 b 4 b 5 a

6D
1
a c

b True: 3, 5; False: 1, 2, 4

2
a
2 It's a good idea to read something in English every day. For example, you can read the BBC news pages on the Internet.
3 Why don't you do something relaxing this evening, such as going for a swim after work?
4 There are more enjoyable ways of preparing for an exam. For example, you could revise with a friend on the same course.
5 You could start a new hobby to help you relax, such as dancing or swimming.

3
a Suggested answer:
Dear Kento
Thanks for your message and I'm glad that you've written to me to ask for some ideas.
I remember when I was learning Japanese, listening was the most difficult thing for me, too. I could understand when my teacher was talking to me, but it was very hard to understand when other people were speaking. Here are some ideas to help you improve your listening in English.
First of all, don't worry if you don't understand every word you hear. That's impossible! You should concentrate only on the most important words.
Secondly, try to get extra listening practice outside the classroom. For instance, you can go to the study centre and practise listening with their CDs, such as the CDs from your Student's Book. You should also listen to the radio in English and watch English or American TV. It's a good idea to watch films with the subtitles.
Next, you can also practise listening to podcasts from the Internet. It's easy to download short stories onto your computer or tablet. Finally, it's a good idea to listen to pop songs while you read the words at the same time. There are lots of internet sites that give you the words of the most popular pop songs.
I hope this helps and please feel free to talk to me after class next week.
Best wishes
Tina

Reading and listening extension
1
a 2 Petra 3 Petra 4 Petra 5 customers 6 Sue

b 2 b 3 a 4 c 5 c

c 2 b 3 a 4 d 5 e

2
a 2 Marsha 3 Max 4 Georgia 5 Max

b 2 c 3 c 4 b 5 b 6 a

Review and extension
1
2 I think he should do some exercise every day.
3 You should read a book to help you relax.
4 She asked me to drive her to the station.
5 My father taught me how to play the guitar.
6 What should I do if I can't sleep very well?

2
2 I was thinking about that TV programme I saw last night.
3 My uncle paid for the tickets and he bought popcorn for us as well.
4 I can't afford to spend a lot of money on a holiday this year.
5 My little sister isn't very interested in fashion.
6 I didn't hear the phone because I was listening to some music.
7 I didn't think that horror film was frightening. What about you?
8 I didn't have any money, so I had to borrow £20 from my brother.

3
2 lent 3 brought 4 wrote 5 paid 6 read 7 sold 8 described

Unit 7

7A
1
a 2 hottest 3 colder 4 cold 5 smallest 6 big 7 larger 8 more expensive

b
2 I think it's the most exciting film I've ever seen.
3 My sister is happier than she's ever been.
4 It's hard to understand her because she speaks more quickly than you.
5 He went to one of the best universities in the USA.
6 The weather's much warmer than it was yesterday.
7 She worked harder than her sister and got 95% in her exam.
8 He speaks English much better now than a year ago. / Now he speaks English much better than a year ago. / He speaks much better English now than a year ago.

2
a 2 get in touch with 3 got a job 4 got to know 5 got together 6 get ill 7 get paid 8 got divorced

b 2 got married 3 got engaged 4 get a place 5 got rich 6 got an offer 7 got to know 8 got paid

7B
1
a 2 f 3 g 4 b 5 d 6 a 7 h 8 e

b 2 put on, healthy 3 gone, lose 4 get 5 gave up 6 overweight 7 allergies 8 smoker

2
a 2 We didn't use to have 3 we didn't use to go 4 we used to invite 5 he used to cook 6 we used to watch 7 used to play 8 didn't use to complain 9 Did you use to live 10 did you use to live

b 2 didn't use to buy 3 did, use to eat 4 used to speak 5 used to go 6 Did, use to play 7 didn't use to have 8 used to watch

7C
1
a 2 g 3 h 4 e 5 f 6 c 7 a 8 b

c 2 hear 3 hurts, get 4 look 5 taking 6 sick 7 you'll 8 problem 9 relief 10 shouldn't

e 6, 8, 3, 1, 5, 4, 2, 7

2

a 2 down 3 up 4 down 5 down 6 up 7 up 8 up

7D

1

a c

b True: 2, 5; False: 1, 3, 4

2

a 2 After 3 Soon 4 a while 5 Then 6 the end

3

a Suggested answer:

About two years ago, I used to travel to work every day by bus. It was an awful journey because of all the traffic and sometimes it took me over an hour to get there. So I decided that I needed to find a quicker way to travel to work. I decided to buy a bicycle. The problem was that I wasn't very fit.

I bought an old bicycle from a friend of mine. At first, I was frightened of cycling on the road with all the cars and lorries. To begin with, I took my bike to the little park near my house every day and cycled very slowly for about five or ten minutes. After a while, I started cycling along the quiet roads to the shops about two kilometres from my house. Then I started cycling the five kilometres from my house to the city centre. In the end I went everywhere on my bicycle!

Now I cycle eight kilometres to work every day and I feel really fit and healthy. It only takes me 30 minutes to get to work, so I save an hour every day.

Reading and listening extension

1

a 2 a 3 d 4 b

b 2 used to be, in the past 3 used to have, in the past 4 used to smoke, in the past 5 are, now

c 2 a 3 c 4 b 5 c

2

a 2 Martin Dowd 3 Stephen Downes 4 Dale George 5 Lisa Baker

b 2 smoking, drinking 3 lost, slimmer / thinner / healthier / fitter 4 married 5 richer / wealthier 6 like

Review and extension

1

2 I think São Paulo is the biggest city in Brazil.
3 My brother didn't use to like coffee when he was a teenager.
4 This exercise is easier than the last one.
5 I'm studying harder this year than last year.
6 London is the most expensive city in the UK.

2

2 You'll have to go on a diet if you want to lose weight.
3 My brother has got a new job and he gets paid very well.
4 She loves her boyfriend and I think they'll get engaged soon.
5 While he was at university, he got to know Sarah.

3

2 h 3 f 4 c 5 b 6 a 7 e 8 d

Unit 8

8A

1

a 2 album 3 classical music 4 architecture 5 novel 6 sculpture 7 photograph 8 film 9 painting 10 TV series

b 2 f 3 d 4 b 5 a 6 g 7 h 8 e

2

a 2 wasn't made / was not made 3 was designed 4 was given 5 were finished 6 were made 7 was designed 8 was found 9 was created 10 were taken 11 was put 12 was finished 13 is visited

b 2 The Eiffel Tower was built in 1889.
3 The novel *Nineteen Eighty-Four* was written in 1949 by George Orwell. / The novel *Nineteen Eighty-Four* was written by George Orwell in 1949.
4 The 2012 Olympic Games were held in London.
5 The film *Schindler's List* was directed by Steven Spielberg in 1993. / The film *Schindler's List* was directed in 1993 by Steven Spielberg.
6 The best coffee is grown in Colombia.
7 Two million new cars were sold in the UK last year. / Two million new cars were sold last year in the UK.
8 5,000 bicycles are produced by this factory every year. / 5,000 bicycles are produced every year by this factory.

8B

1

a 1 **B** 've loved / have loved, since
2 **A** Have you lived, for **B** 've lived / have lived
3 **A** have you been **B** 've been / have been, since, 've known / have known, for
4 **A** have you had **B** 've had / have had, since
5 **A** have you worked **B** 've been / have been, for

b 2 've known 3 's been 4 's had 5 've been, worked 6 's had

2

a play: squash, golf, volleyball, tennis, football, ice hockey, rugby
go: surfing, snowboarding, ice skating, jogging, rock climbing, skateboarding, scuba diving, windsurfing
do: yoga, athletics, judo, aerobics, karate

c Across: 8 windsurfing 10 skating 11 climbing 12 yoga; Down: 1 hockey 2 snowboarding 3 athletics 4 golf 6 surfing 7 jogging 9 diving

3

a 2 b 3 a 4 b 5 a

8C

1

a 2 I'm sorry, I couldn't come to your party yesterday because I was ill.
3 I couldn't email you because my computer wasn't working.
4 I didn't mean to be late for the meeting, but my watch is broken.
5 I'm really sorry I haven't bought you a present, but the shops were closed.
6 I'm sorry I didn't call you last night, but my mobile wasn't working.
7 I was going to finish the report by today, but I've been so busy.
8 I meant to send you a birthday card, but I couldn't find your address.

b 2 couldn't 3 mean 4 matter, fine 5 going to 6 meant 7 worry, fault 8 had to

2

a 2 down 3 up 4 down 5 down 6 up 7 up 8 down

8D

1

a c

b True: 1, 4, 5; False: 2, 3

2

a 2 However 3 although 4 However 5 Although 6 although

3

a Suggested answer:

War Horse by Michael Morpurgo is the story of Joey, a horse that is sold to the British Army at the beginning of the First World War. He is sent to France and is ridden by Captain Nicholls. However, Captain Nicholls is killed in the fighting and Joey is given to a younger soldier called Warren. While he is with Warren, Joey becomes friends with another horse called Topthorn and they have lots of adventures during the war. Later in the story, Joey and Topthorn are taken by the Germans. Topthorn is killed, but Joey works for the German army until the end of the war.

Although this book was written for children, I really enjoyed it. The story is very interesting and the characters are described very well. You can really imagine what the First World War was like. It's a beautiful story, although it's also very sad and it made me cry. However, there is a happy ending because at the end of the war Joey is returned to Albert, who was his original owner before he was sold to the army. I couldn't put the book down until I got to the end and I can definitely recommend it.

Reading and listening extension

1

a True: 1, 2, 5; False: 3, 4

b 2 Sam Lee 3 *To Sleep To Dream* 4 *Flathampton* 5 *To Sleep To Dream, Flathampton*

c 2 a 3 c 4 b 5 a

Answer key

2
a 2 Stirling Ranges 3 Margaret River 4 Bunbury 5 near Fremantle
6 Stirling Ranges, Bunbury, Margaret River

b 2 The sea 3 film directors 4 listen to 5 Jenny

Review and extension

1
2 I have known Tanya since I was a child. / I've known Tanya since I was a child.
3 We've lived in Berlin for more than 10 years.
4 St Paul's Cathedral was designed by Christopher Wren.
5 I taught at that university from 2010 to 2013.
6 I have played golf since I was twelve years old.

2
2 Skateboarding is a great way for children to get fit.
3 Have you got a photograph of your girlfriend?
4 Let's play golf this afternoon.
5 These days, ice skating is popular in London during the winter.
6 When I was at school, I had to do gymnastics every Wednesday.
7 The *Mona Lisa* is one of the most famous paintings in the world.
8 Let's go surfing at the beach this afternoon.

3
2 the way 3 mistake 4 bus 5 heart 6 hand 7 far 8 next Monday

Unit 9

9A

1
a Across: 6 Law 7 Management 8 Psychology; Down: 1 Education 2 Art 4 Medicine 5 Engineering

b 2 degree 3 essays 4 fail 5 revise 6 handed 7 notes 8 place 9 get 10 pass

2
a 2 I'll go to the USA on holiday if I can find a cheap flight.
3 If they revise every day, they might pass their exams.
4 If she does well in her exams, she might get a place at Cambridge University.
5 She'll have to get excellent grades if she wants to study Medicine at university.
6 I'll call him tomorrow morning if he doesn't reply to my email tonight.
7 Your teacher might give you a bad mark if you don't hand in your essay on time.
8 If you fail your exams, you won't get into university.

3
a 2 If you take notes in the lesson, // it will be easier to revise for the exam.
3 I'm going to work harder next year // so that I get better grades.
4 If she fails her exam, // she'll have to take it again in January.
5 Although he got excellent grades, // he didn't get a place at Oxford University.

9B

1
a 2 not to take 3 trying 4 to see 5 not to fail 6 not having 7 to speak 8 to go 9 spending 10 not doing

b 2 to take 3 going 4 to get 5 playing / to play 6 to meet 7 reading 8 snowing / to snow

2
a 2 recommended 3 disliked 4 forgot 5 agreed 6 imagined 7 missed 8 avoid 9 managed 10 regretted 11 seemed 12 refused

b 2 avoids 3 arrange 4 forgot 5 recommends 6 miss 7 refuse 8 disliked 9 seems 10 manage

9C

1
a 9, 7, 3, 2, 5, 4, 8, 1, 6, 10

c 2 it is 3 it's 4 good time 5 catch that 6 just saying 7 I've got 8 call you back 9 got to go 10 Ring 11 soon

2
a 2 a 3 a 4 b 5 a 6 b

9D

1
a c

b True: 1, 3; False: 2, 4, 5

2
a 2 They 3 She's 4 her 5 one 6 He, he 7 us 8 It, it

3
a Suggested answer:
Tell us about you …
Hello everyone. I'm Hitomi and I come from Osaka, in Japan. I'm doing a Master's Degree in Economics at Tokyo University and next year I want to get a job in London or New York. I studied English for ten years at school, so I can write it quite well, but I can't speak it very well, so I need to practise!
How do you feel about this course?
I really want to learn more about American cinema because I've always loved watching American films. I hope the course will help me to improve my English. I'm looking forward to talking about all the films we're going to watch with the other students on the course (via Skype?). I'm sure my English will improve quickly during the course.
What do you do when you're not studying?
When I'm not studying, I play a lot of sport. I play tennis once or twice a week and sometimes golf at weekends. I also go to the gym at the university because I like keeping really fit. Sometimes I do yoga when I feel stressed. It really helps me to relax.

Reading and listening extension

1
a 2 Medicine 3 Law 4 Psychology

b 2 c 3 a 4 b 5 b

c 2 Britain 3 speaks 4 studying 5 work

2
a True: 1, 2, 6; False: 3, 4, 5

b 2 f 3 e 4 a 5 c 6 d

Review and extension

1
2 I want you to buy me some bread and milk from the shop.
3 We won't play golf this afternoon if it rains.
4 She enjoys reading books about dinosaurs.
5 Will you go to university next year if you get good grades?
6 I've just finished having dinner with my family.

2
2 He did really well at school and got into a good university.
3 She got a very bad mark for her last History essay.
4 Although they worked hard, they both failed their Maths exam.
5 She always took taxis because she disliked waiting for buses.
6 He did a degree in Medicine and now he's a doctor. / He took a degree in Medicine and now he's a doctor.

3
2 up 3 through 4 down 5 off 6 on

Unit 10

10A

1
a 2 Would you complain if the waiter made a mistake with your bill?
3 What would you do if there were no teachers at school?
4 If I cycled to work, I could save a lot of money on petrol.
5 I would feel less stressed if I did yoga every day.
6 If I missed the last bus, I'd have to take a taxi.
7 I could stop working if I became rich.
8 If you found the film on the Internet, would you download it?

b 2 Could you work, needed
3 was, I'd complain
4 I could take, wasn't
5 walked, you'd feel
6 stopped, 'd take
7 wouldn't walk, were
8 would you do, lost

2
a 2 g 3 d 4 c 5 f 6 e 7 b 8 a
b 2 off 3 round 4 like 5 up 6 in 7 after 8 on

3
a 2 unstressed 3 stressed 4 stressed 5 unstressed 6 stressed

10B
1
a 2 a little 3 no 4 much 5 much 6 many 7 many 8 any 9 a few 10 any 11 some

b 2 too much 3 enough milk 4 too 5 clearly enough 6 too many 7 too quickly 8 big enough

2
a Across: 5 decision 8 delivered 9 complaint 10 complain;
Down: 1 choose 2 decided 4 description 6 queue 7 explain

3
a 2 b 3 b 4 a 5 b 6 a 7 b 8 b

10C
1
a 7, 1, 4, 2, 6, 5, 8, 3

c 2 I'll ask someone to look at that for you right away.
3 We've been here for over an hour, but we still haven't ordered.
4 These shoes don't fit me because they're a bit small.
5 I've changed my mind and I've decided to keep it.
6 I'd like to exchange it for something else.
7 I'd like to return this watch, please.
8 I'll give you a full refund.
9 Your sales assistant hasn't been very helpful.

2
a 2 b 3 a 4 b 5 b 6 a 7 b 8 a

10D
1
a 1 Email C 2 Email A 3 Email B

b True: 1, 4; False: 2, 3, 5

2
a 2 Thank you very much for your email of 15 June.
3 I am writing to apologise for the poor service you received in our restaurant last Saturday.
4 We have just opened the restaurant and we have had a few problems finding experienced waiters and waitresses.
5 However, we are working hard to improve our levels of service and I am confident that we will not have any more problems of this kind in the future.
6 We hope you will come back to our restaurant again and we would like to offer you a 50% discount on your next meal with us.
7 This is our way of apologising for the problems you have had.
8 Yours sincerely,

3
a Suggested answer:
Dear Mr Hurst
Thank you for your email of 10 July about the problems you had during your stay at our hotel. I am writing to apologise for the poor service you had while you were staying with us.
Unfortunately, we have had a few problems with our website recently. I think that is why you were not given a room with a view of the sea. We have also had some problems with our water heating system in the last few weeks, so this is why sometimes there was not enough hot water for showers or baths. Finally, we did not have enough staff in our restaurant while you were staying with us because three of our waiters became ill.
I hope you will come and stay at our hotel in Sorrento again. I would like to offer you a 50% discount the next time you come to the Hotel Dante. This is our way of apologising for the problems you have had.
Yours faithfully
Enzo Conte
Manager
Hotel Dante

Reading and listening extension
1
a 2 c 3 a
b 2 a 3 b 4 a 5 b
c 2 b 3 b 4 c 5 a 6 a,b 7 c 8 c

2
a 2 Zuza 3 Zuza 4 No one 5 Haluk 6 Zuza
b 2 c 3 c 4 b 5 b 6 c

Review and extension
1
2 He invited too many people to his party – over 100!
3 If I had a motorbike, I wouldn't take the bus to work.
4 This morning it was too cold to swim in the sea.
5 I would go on a diet if I were overweight. / I'd go on a diet if I were overweight.
6 If Chile won the World Cup, he would be delighted.

2
2 Tim isn't here at the moment, but I can pass on a message.
3 There's a very small menu in that restaurant, so the choice of food is very limited.
4 It's sad that Anna and Steven have broken up after being together for ten years.
5 If you aren't happy with your hotel, you should make a complaint. / If you aren't happy with your hotel, you should complain.
6 She was offered a better job, but turned it down.

3
2 go 3 put 4 keeps 5 put 6 carry 7 got 8 kept

Unit 11
11A
1
a 2 where 3 which 4 who 5 where 6 who 7 which 8 which 9 where 10 who

b 2 There's a woman over there that used to work for your company. / There's a woman over there who used to work for your company.
3 There's a café near me which has 50 different kinds of tea! / There's a café near me that has 50 different kinds of tea!
4 My dad's got a cousin in Houston who works for NASA. / My dad's got a cousin in Houston that works for NASA.
5 I know an Italian restaurant in London where you can have chocolate spaghetti!
6 I've got a new camera which also takes video pictures. / I've got a new camera that also takes video pictures.
7 That's the cinema where they're showing the new James Bond film next week.
8 He's just bought a new TV which gives you access to the Internet. / He's just bought a new TV that gives you access to the Internet.

2
a Across: 4 tea bag 6 street 10 car park 11 rock star 12 centre;
Down: 1 coffee 3 ticket 5 address 7 TV screen 8 machine 9 games

3
a 2 com<u>pu</u>ter screen 3 science <u>fic</u>tion 4 a<u>dd</u>ress book 5 <u>bread</u> knife 6 <u>car</u> park 7 <u>co</u>ffee cup 8 <u>book</u>shelf

11B
1
a 2 a 3 a 4 Ø 5 a 6 the 7 an 8 Ø 9 Ø 10 the 11 a 12 the 13 Ø 14 Ø 15 the 16 Ø 17 the 18 the 19 the 20 Ø 21 the 22 a / the

b 2 In the UK, police officers don't usually carry guns.
3 I love Italian ice cream. It's the best in the world!
4 They drove to Paris by car and then stayed in a lovely hotel near the Eiffel Tower.
5 France is the most popular country for tourists in the world.
6 Doctors in the USA are paid much more than nurses.

2
a 2 g 3 a 4 d 5 b 6 e 7 h 8 c

b 2 Unfortunately 3 by chance 4 Luckily 5 on purpose 6 Amazingly

94

Answer key

3

a 2a 3b 4b 5a 6b 7a 8a 9b

11C

1

a 4, 6, 1, 3, 5, 2

c
2 Go through those doors and then down the corridor.
3 So, first go along the corridor to the stairs?
4 Could you tell me where the staff restaurant is, please?
5 Then go down the corridor and it's the first office on the right.
6 Go up the stairs to the third floor.
7 So, can I just check?
8 Right, I think I've got that.
9 At the top of the stairs, turn right and go along another corridor.
10 The meeting room is the second door on the left.

2

a 2 fur 3 sir 4 short 5 ward 6 earl 7 Paul 8 worm

11D

1

a b

b True: 1, 3, 5; False: 2, 4

2

a 2 as 3 because 4 because of 5 As 6 as a result of
7 Because of 8 because

3

a Suggested answer:
In my view, the most important invention of the last 25 years has been the mobile phone. Before it was invented, if you wanted to speak to somebody on the phone, you had to be at home, in the office or in a public phone box. With a mobile phone it is much easier to keep in contact with your friends, your family and your work colleagues than before. Because it is a mobile, you can have a conversation wherever you are – in the street, at the supermarket, in a car or on a train. Because of this, it is also easier for people to stay in touch with their children or with their elderly relatives. It is also very useful to have a mobile phone if you have an accident or if you need to call the police. These days, mobile phones are not only devices that let you make phone calls and send texts. You can also take photos, record videos, listen to music, surf the Internet and talk to your friends on Facebook. I believe it's the most useful thing I have. In fact, I don't know where I would be without it.

Reading and listening extension

1

a 2 plane / aeroplane 3 rainforest / forest 4 sweets 5 river 6 boat 7 hospital

b True: 1, 2; False: 3, 4, 5

c 2 b 3 e 4 c 5 a 6 f

2

a 5, 3, 6, 7, 4, 2, 1

b 2 a 3 c 4 a 5 b 6 b

Review and extension

1

2 Sorry, I can't talk to you right now because I'm at work.
3 Generally speaking, most men like watching sport on TV.
4 Modern Living is the shop where I bought my leather sofa.
5 Look! That's the man who stole my wallet!
6 John F. Kennedy was the American president who was assassinated in Dallas in 1963. / John F. Kennedy was the American president that was assassinated in Dallas in 1963.

2

2 I think I wrote his phone number in my address book.
3 Surprisingly, it tasted a bit like chicken.
4 I'm afraid of heights, so I don't want to go rock climbing.
5 He opened the car door without looking and hit an old man on a bicycle.
6 I'm sorry I broke your coffee cup – it was an accident.

3

2 a 3 e 4 d 5 b 6 c

Unit 12

12A

1

a Across: 5 camel 6 bee 7 parrot; Down: 1 spider 2 gorilla 4 whale 8 tiger

2

a 2 had, finished 3 had worked 4 had got up 5 had, begun 6 had stolen
7 had missed 8 had stopped

b 2 began 3 left 4 was 5 had crashed 6 was 7 reached 8 had missed
9 had taken 10 arrived 11 tried 12 had sold 13 bought 14 spent
15 landed 16 didn't collect 17 had been 18 found 19 had closed
20 went

3

a Sound 1 come, done, run, won Sound 2 fallen, taught
Sound 3 known, spoken, woken

12B

1

a
2 said, she would, me
3 told me, her, was watching, her
4 said, they'd been, their
5 told him, his, couldn't, them
6 told us, thought, they would go, their
7 said, she'd already done, her
8 told us, his, wasn't going to, his

b
2 He told me he would invite us to his house for dinner next week. / He told me that he would invite us to his house for dinner next week.
3 She told James he could use her tablet to do his homework. / She told James that he could use her tablet to do his homework.
4 He said the traffic had been really bad, so they had missed the 17:15 train. / He said that the traffic had been really bad, so they had missed the 17:15 train.
5 She told me they were going to buy me a lovely present for my birthday. / She told me that they were going to buy me a lovely present for my birthday.
6 He said he had just tried calling his friend, but she hadn't replied, so he thought she was away on holiday. / He said that he had just tried calling his friend, but she hadn't replied, so he thought she was away on holiday.

2

a Across: 5 sociable 7 serious 8 shy 10 anxious; Down: 1 careless
3 selfish 4 generous 6 creative 9 funny

3

a 2 a 3 a 4 b 5 b 6 a 7 a 8 a 9 a 10 b

12C

1

a 2 d 3 e 4 c 5 a 6 b 7 h 8 f

c 2 B You're absolutely right. 3 B Definitely. 4 B Oh, please.
5 B That's true. 6 B You're right.

2

a 2 Italian 3 British 4 San Francisco 5 Barcelona 6 American football

12D

1

a d

b True: 2, 4; False: 1, 3, 5

2

a 2 Later that day 3 The following morning 4 Suddenly
5 A few minutes later

3

a Suggested answer:
Last year, I went on a walking holiday in Scotland with three of my friends. We had only been there for a day when the accident happened. We had just got to the top of a mountain and we were having some sandwiches that we'd made for lunch. Suddenly, the weather changed completely. It had been a clear, sunny day when we left the village where we were staying. However, now it was snowing heavily and you could only see clearly for about 20 metres. We started walking down the path towards the next village where we were going to spend the night. The snow was getting deeper, so we walked slowly down the mountain. All of us were confident walkers, so we didn't think we would

95

have any problems. Suddenly, I heard a shout from behind me. When I turned round, my friend Anthony was lying on the ground. He said that he had fallen over a rock. As soon as I saw him, I knew it was serious. He said his leg was hurting badly and that he thought he had broken it. We decided to call for help. Fortunately, my mobile phone was getting a signal, so I managed to call the emergency services.

After a short time, the mountain rescue team arrived in their helicopter. They landed very close to where we were. They carried Anthony to the helicopter and we all got in with him. Ten minutes later, we arrived at the hospital. Luckily, Anthony's leg wasn't badly broken and they didn't need to operate. We all felt very relieved.

David

Reading and listening extension

1

a 4, 1, 5, 2, 6, 3

b 2 anxious, was worried about changing something
3 generous, gave lots of money to buy something
4 sociable, friendly with people

c 2 a   3 b   4 c

2

a 6, 5, 1, 8, 4, 7, 2, 3

b 2 a   3 b   4 b   5 a   6 b

Review and extension

1

2 I told her that she couldn't go to the beach by herself. / I told her she couldn't go to the beach by herself. / I said that she couldn't go to the beach by herself. / I said she couldn't go to the beach by herself.
3 He told me that my mother had called earlier that day. / He told me my mother had called earlier that day. / He said that my mother had called earlier that day. / He said my mother had called earlier that day.
4 We told her that her father wouldn't buy her a new computer. / We told her her father wouldn't buy her a new computer. / We said that her father wouldn't buy her a new computer. / We said her father wouldn't buy her a new computer.
5 Tom had never ridden a camel before, so he was rather nervous.
6 Our train had already left when we finally arrived at the station.

2

2 She's a really honest person. If shop assistants give her too much change, she always tells them.
3 He's very easy going. I'm sure he won't mind if you bring your friend with you when you go to his house for dinner.
4 I'm not a very confident person. For example, I don't like speaking when I'm in a meeting with a large group of people.
5 Teachers have to learn to be patient with their students because sometimes they don't learn things immediately.
6 Why are you always so careless! You've already lost your mobile phone twice this year!

3

2 At your age   3 old age   4 apart in age   5 at an early age
6 about my age

Vox pop video

Unit 1

a 2 through cycling   3 through friends   4 at language classes or dance classes
5 on trains or buses

b 2 c   3 d   4 a

c 2 a   3 b   4 a   5 c   6 a

Unit 2

a 2 b   3 b   4 a

b 2 b   3 c   4 a

c 2 c   3 a   4 b

Unit 3

a 2 Darren   3 Carolyn   4 Colin

b 2 six months ago   3 doesn't usually buy

c 2 c   3 b   4 a

Unit 4

a 2 b   3 c   4 a

b 2 meal with her friends   3 barbecue with her family   4 doesn't celebrate

c 2 c   3 d   4 a

Unit 5

a 2 b   3 c   4 a

b 2 talking to   3 friendly   4 science

c 2 c   3 d   4 a

Unit 6

a 2 c   3 a   4 b

b 2 Maibritt   3 Colin   4 Mark

c 2 b   3 a   4 c

Unit 7

a 2 a   3 b

b 1 Laurence   2 Darren   3 Peter

c 1 c   2 c   3 b

Unit 8

a 2 b   3 a

b 2 d   3 b   4 a

c 2 c   3 b   4 a

Unit 9

a 2 a   3 d   4 b

b 2 c   3 b   4 b

c 2 Carolyn   3 Matt   4 Lauren

Unit 10

a 2 b   3 b   4 c

b 2 c   3 b   4 b   5 a

c 2 would change seats   3 after five minutes   4 the people themselves
5 people that were making the noise

Unit 11

a 1 Dee Dee   2 Petros   3 James

b 2 d   3 a   4 b

c 2 b   3 a   4 c

Unit 12

a 2 d   3 b   4 e   5 a

b 2 b   3 a   4 c

c 2 b   3 a   4 b   5 a